Presented to

_____

From

_____

Date

_____

*"At each and every sunrise you will hear my voice
as I prepare my sacrifice of prayer to you.
Every morning I lay out the pieces of my life on the altar
and wait for your fire to fall upon my heart."
Psalms 5:3 (TPT)*

31 Day Devotional

She MEANS BUSINESS

Faith & Prosperity for Women in Business

MARGO BUSH

bush
PUBLISHING
& associates

Unless otherwise indicated, all Scripture quotations are taken from the New King James Version of the Bible, copyright © 1979, 1980, 1982, Thomas Nelson, Inc., Publishers.

All Scripture quotations marked KJV are taken from the King James Version of the Bible.

Scripture quotations marked TPT are from The Passion Translation®. Copyright © 2017, 2018, 2020 by Passion & Fire Ministries, Inc. Used by permission. All rights reserved. ThePassionTranslation.com.

All Scripture quotations are taken from The Message, copyright © 1993, 2002, 2018 by Eugene H. Peterson. Used by permission of NavPress. All rights reserved. Represented by Tyndale House Publishers.

Scripture quotations taken from the Amplified® Bible (AMP), Copyright © 2015 by The Lockman Foundation. Used by permission. www.Lockman.org

Scripture quotations taken from The Holy Bible, New International Version®, NIV®. Copyright © 1973, 1978, 1984, 2011 by Biblica, Inc. Used with permission of Zondervan. All rights reserved worldwide. www.zondervan.com

31 Day Devotional

SHE MEANS BUSINESS

Faith & Prosperity for Women in Business

ISBN: 978-1-944566-83-8 (Print Edition)

ISBN: 978-1-944566-84-5 (E-Book Edition)

Copyright © 2026 Bush Publishing & Associates

Bush Publishing & Associates, LLC books may be ordered at everywhere and at Amazon.com.

For further information, please contact:

Bush Publishing & Associates

Tulsa, Oklahoma

www.bushpublishing.com

Produced and printed in the United States of America.

No portion of this book may be used or reproduced by any means: graphic, electronic or mechanical, including photocopying, recording, taping, or by any information storage retrieval system, without the written permission of the publisher, except in the case of brief quotations embodied in critical articles and reviews.

DEDICATION

I dedicate this book to you, Mom, in deep appreciation for your love and encouragement as I've followed the path God has set before me. You have been a wonderful mother—always supporting my dreams, standing by me, and urging me to keep moving forward when the road felt long. Even when the path I chose wasn't clear to you, you still encouraged me to press on.

When Bill died and I was only forty-nine—convinced my life was over—you were there, reassuring me that there were still many years ahead to rebuild. Your words still echo in my ears today:

> *"You don't know how young you really are. You have so many years to do what God has placed in your heart and fulfill your dreams."*

You don't know how many times I've drawn strength from those words to take the next big assignment God has given me. Because of them, I've rebuilt my life—and it has been so rewarding.

Mom, because of your encouragement, prayers, and hands-on help along the way, I am now launching my fourth (and final—I think—LOL!) business and publishing my fourth book this year—with many more to come.

> *Her children arise up, and call her blessed...*
>
> —PROVERBS 31:28

I call you blessed, Mom. Thank you again for the love and encouragement you've poured into my journey. You were the reason I went to Bible College. You and I both know—it changed everything.

I believe every child deserves a mom like you.

I love you!

Your daughter,

—Margo

"Big dreams require big faith, and God is the partner who makes them possible."

—Dr. Margo Bush

Table of Contents

Foreward xv
Preface xvii
Introduction xxi
She Walks in Wealth 25
She Has a Plan 31
She Increases 37
She Prospers 45
She Finds Favor 51
She Waits Upon Him 57
She Walks in Wisdom 61
She's a Million Dollar Mom 65
She Is Diligent 71
She Buys a Field 77
She Steps Into Overflow 83
She's Ready 89
She Faces Heaven 97
Alabaster Box 103
She Has a Kingdom-Mindset 109
She Steps Into Abundance 117
Her Million Dollar Challenge 125
Women of Victory 133
Her Gift Opens Doors 137
Her Divine Partner 143
She Is Exquisite 149
Woman of Wealth, Wisdom, and the Word 153
She Knows How to Prosper 157
She Believes and She Speaks 163
She is a Successful Businesswoman 167
Her Gift Opens Doors 171
For Such a Time as This She Lives 177
She Is Leading in the Marketplace 181
She Masters Her Time 187
Her Mission in the Marketplace 195
She Means Business 201
She Walks in Great Blessing 211
About the Author 217
Recommended Reading 223

Foreward

When I first met Margo, I immediately recognized the gift of God and the passion within her—not only to achieve her own goals, but to help other women bring their dreams to life and experience success in business. *She Means Business: Faith & Prosperity for Women in Business* is a timely and powerful invitation for women to awaken that vision and boldly bring it into fulfillment.

Margo Bush writes not only as an entrepreneur and author, but as a woman who understands the purpose and perseverance required to walk in prosperity. Through this 31-day devotional, she walks alongside the reader with wisdom, warmth, and practical instruction, helping transform ideas into businesses that succeed. Each day is filled with encouragement and tools designed to build confidence, strengthen resolve, and inspire action—moving women from the dream stage into tangible results.

Ephesians 2:10 declares it beautifully in The Passion Translation:

> *"We have become his poetry, a re-created people that will fulfill the destiny he has given each of us…Even before we were born, God planned in advance our destiny and the good works we would do to fulfill it."*

This truth resonates throughout the pages of this book. You are God's poetry—created with intention, designed for impact, and equipped to prosper in the work He has prepared for you.

Any woman who reads and applies the principles Margo Bush has so effectively penned will discover that what once felt like a distant dream can become a thriving, purpose-filled business. May this devotional stir your faith, sharpen your vision, and empower you to step confidently into all that God has destined you to build.

Trina Hankins

Pastor | Speaker | Author of *God's Healing Word*

Preface

Why I Wrote This Book

I wrote *She Means Business* for the woman who knows she is called to more—but has quietly wondered if wanting more is somehow wrong.

For years, I have worked with women who love God deeply, serve faithfully, and carry big dreams in their hearts. They are gifted, capable, and full of vision—yet many of them struggle with permission. Permission to grow. Permission to earn more. Permission to build something significant without feeling prideful, selfish, or out of alignment with their faith.

I've watched women downplay their brilliance, shrink their goals, and apologize for their ambition—in the marketplace and in ministry. Not because they lack ability, but because no one ever taught them that business is a calling, wealth is stewardship, and success is in Kingdom alignment with scripture

She Means Business was born out of that tension.

Through my years as a minister, pastor, business coach, entrepreneur, and publisher, I have heard countless stories of women who have overcome loss, failure, addiction, betrayal, financial hardship, and fear—yet still felt uncertain about how to build a profitable, sustainable business that honors God. I realized something powerful: testimony alone is not enough. Women don't just need inspiration—they need education, strategy, and biblical principles that help them thrive in their field of favor.

This book is not about chasing money.

It is about understanding what God says about making money, so it no longer works against you.

It is about building businesses with intention, excellence, and faith for Kingdom Impact.

It is about breaking the cycle of survival and stepping into overflow—so you can fund vision, support others, and leave a legacy.

Inside these pages, you will find encouragement, practical wisdom, and faith-filled truth designed to help you think differently about business, money, and your God-given potential. You will be challenged to grow—not just spiritually, but strategically. To stop playing small. To stop waiting. To stop doubting whether you are "qualified enough" to build what God has placed inside you.

This book is meant to serve as a daily devotional so you can repeat the teaching, motivation and inspiration every 31 days.

I believe that if you are reading this book, it is not by accident.

You were created to build–a business, a ministry, a life filled with purpose.

And you were entrusted with influence—in ministry, the marketplace or both.

She Means Business is your reminder that faith and success are not opposites. When aligned with God, they work together to create impact far beyond yourself.

This is your season to rise with confidence.

To build with clarity.

To earn with intention.

And to walk boldly in your God-given assignment.

You don't just have a dream.

Preface

You carry a mandate—and mindset is the doorway to prosperity.

There is more for you to build, more for you to earn, and more God wants to release through you,

because Heaven already knows—**she means business**.

You can do it—I believe in you,

—Dr. Margo Bush

Introduction

Welcome, extraordinary businesswoman!

As a woman entrepreneur, you face unique challenges—balancing faith, family, business, and personal growth. Yet, God has called you to increase in all areas of your life, using your gifts, talents, and influence—fulfilling your God-given dreams.

These daily devotionals and scripture verses will show you how to build a successful business, how God thinks about wealth and prosperity, and most importantly, how you should think about building a business that helps you earn more, create financial security and advance the Kingdom. In my life, I have had to fight to overcome a 'Lack Mindset'. That wealth and prosperity was for someone else but not me and my family. Don't get me wrong, we have never really lacked, but it was always scarcity. The scriptures in this book are what I meditated on, said out loud to myself daily—yes daily, confessed over my business, my family, and my life, until I got it in my heart that God didn't see money as anything but a tool and His covenant promise to me. Wealth was not something to attain to, but that it was already mine through sonship (daughtership). The ability to earn more in my business, provide financial security, and to use what I earn for Kingdom impact. The truth is that 90% of building a prosperous business is mindset. Needless to say, I didn't have the proper mindset to grow a thriving, wildly successful business when I started. Let's become women of wisdom and see Deuteronomy 8:18 and 3 John 2 come to pass in our business and life. Growing a business that glorifies God, serves people, and advances the Kingdom.

> *"Wise people (women) are builders–they (we) build families, businesses, communities. And through intelligence and insight their (our) enterprises are established and endure. Because of their (our) skilled leadership, the hearts' of people (our employees, customers and clients) are filled, with the treasures of wisdom and the pleasures of spiritual wealth."*
>
> —Proverbs 24:3-4 (TPT)

Each daily devotion shows consistent themes:

- Business built on **wisdom, integrity, and character** tends to endure.

- **Diligence, planning, foresight**, and avoiding procrastination are repeatedly encouraged.

- **Fairness, just measures, honoring agreements** are seen not as optional, but required.

- **Seeking counsel, humility, trusting God** are essential for navigating risk and growth.

- The "virtuous woman" of **Proverbs 31** offers a poetic model of a successful, generous, industrious enterprise.

This 31-Day Devotional is designed to strengthen your faith, cultivate a mindset of wealth, wisdom, and prosperity, to equip you with a foundation of biblical principles to build a wildly successful business.

Each day includes:

- **Scripture** to inspire and guide you.

- **Devotional** applying the Word to your business life.

- **Faith Action** to put God's principles into practice.

- **Prayer Prompt** to connect with God, and declare His promises.

Introduction

Commit to 31 days of intentional growth and wisdom from the scriptures, and watch God transform your faith, finances, and opportunities.

> "At each and every sunrise you will hear my voice as I prepare my *sacrifice of prayer* to you. Every morning I lay out the pieces of my life on the altar and wait *for your fire to fall upon my heart*."
>
> —Psalms 5:3

With scriptures, daily devotional, guided reflections, powerful Faith Actions, and additional scripture translations for each day, this book will help you renew your mind, strengthen your spirit, and unlock the prosperity mindset to build a strong and lasting life and business.

Discover how to:

- Build a business rooted in faith and integrity.
- Attract divine connections and opportunities.
- Operate in fearless confidence and excellence.
- See your work as worship and your business as ministry.
- Gain wisdom and learn how to earn more, create financial security, and have Kingdom Impact.

Whether you're just starting out or scaling your business to new heights, *SHE MEANS BUSINESS* will empower you to follow His divine wisdom, gain business strategy, and know your covenant rights for wealth and prosperity—to grow a business God's way.

It's time to stop playing small. You were created for greatness—and SHE MEANS BUSINESS.

SHE WALKS IN WEALTH

But thou shalt remember the LORD thy God: for it is He that giveth thee power to get wealth, that He may establish His covenant which He sware unto thy fathers, as it is this day.

—DEUTERONOMY 8:18

DEVOTIONAL

God has given you the power to build a thriving organization. It is He who can bring you favor among men when no one else can. When it seems like all else fails, it is He who brings new life to a problem, an issue, or a contract. You are not alone in the work of growing your business—if you remember the Lord who gave it all to you.

You may have thought it was just you—grinding, hustling, doing everything you can to make it happen. But it's not just you. You have a divine business partner—*the Lord Himself*. Act like it, talk to Him, and call on Him. He wants to lead you into success!

He is the best partner you could ever have. He holds the wisdom you need, the direction you've been praying for, and the timing for every decision. He knows when to expand, where to build, and what products to develop. The same God who created heaven and earth has given you the power to earn more, create financial security for you and your family, and to teach you how to effect the Kingdom.

But this power requires using your faith—faith to believe that what He said in Deuteronomy 8:18 is true for you: *"...for it is He that gives you the power..."* (NKJV). Remember Him in every decision, every transaction, every investment. Invite Him into your boardroom, your calendar, and your strategy meetings. When you do, you're not just running a business—*you're operating under divine partnership.*

The Message Translation says:

> *If you start thinking to yourselves, 'I did all this. And all by myself. I'm rich. It's all mine!'—well, think again. Remember that God, your God, gave you the strength to produce all this wealth so as to confirm the covenant that He promised to your ancestors—as it is today.*
>
> —Deuteronomy 8:17–18 (MSG)

And the Amplified Translation declares:

> *But you shall remember [with profound respect] the Lord your God, for it is He who is giving you power to make wealth, that He may confirm His covenant which He swore (solemnly promised) to your fathers, as it is this day.*
>
> —Deuteronomy 8:18 (AMP)

When I took over our book publishing company after my husband died, I honestly did not know the first thing about how to grow a business. All I had known were the four walls of a church. I had been a minister's wife since I was twenty, fresh out of Bible college. No one had ever taught me how to make money or grow an organization.

There I was, taking over a small business with children still in high school. How was I going to support them, myself, and the employees we had? I had no résumé, no boss on this planet to recommend me, and no experience I felt would translate into corporate earnings. So—*I turned to the Word.*

The Lord said He would supply all my needs—and at that moment, I needed wisdom to build. He led me, opened doors, brought the right people, and taught me how to build. Within three months, I was tripling my profits, and by the end of the second year, I had paid off all the equipment in a 4,200 sq. ft. printing and publishing company. He is faithful to teach you how to do what He has assigned you to do. As you use your faith and speak the Word, you'll watch your business thrive and grow in ways beyond your wildest dreams!

The second part of this verse is one of the most powerful truths you can stand on:

> *"...that He may establish His covenant which He swore to your fathers, as it is this day."*
>
> —DEUTERONOMY 8:18

Why does God give you the power to create wealth? So that His covenant—His promise—can be established on the earth. It's not random that you're building a business. It's not just a personal dream. It's part of His divine plan to bring wealth to His people. It is His promise—your covenant right.

You are part of something bigger—something eternal. God has sworn to establish His covenant, and He has chosen you as one of the vessels through which He will do it. (See Deuteronomy 7:8–12)

You are anointed and appointed for such a time as this—to be a successful entrepreneur, to earn more, to create financial security, and to advance the Kingdom. You are not doing business alone. You are partnering with the Creator of all things, who delights in seeing you prosper. (See 3 John 1:2)

Along the way, you'll sense gentle nudges from the Holy Spirit—that still, small voice saying, *"Go this way,"* or *"Wait,"* or *"Hire him or her."* In the natural, it might seem like an odd choice, but trust the leading. That is your business partner—*the Holy Spirit*—guiding you into all truth and success.

MEANS BUSINESS

When you don't know what to do, talk to Him. Don't leave Him out! He'll place you in the right rooms, at the right time, with the right people. *Expect divine connections.* Expect unexpected doors to open. Expect favor in boardrooms where you may feel least qualified—because He is establishing His covenant through you.

Do you see it now? This is bigger than just your dream—it is His success story for you. Your business is a vehicle through which God is fulfilling His promises on earth. When you remember that—when you remember Him—He will lead you into wealth and prosperity, not just for your benefit—*but for His glory.*

Declare each day as your feet hit the floor:

> *"Today, I remember the Lord my God, for it is He who gives me the power to create wealth. I partner with You, Lord, in every decision I make today, and together, we establish Your covenant promises on the earth."*

> *"Your business is a vehicle through which God is fulfilling His covenant on earth through you."*

—Dr. Margo Bush

Faith Action

Invite God into your business today. Before you make another decision, pause and pray, *"Lord, what do You say about this?"* Review your goals, projects, or partnerships and ask the Holy Spirit for direction. Write down one area where you need His wisdom, and expect divine instruction.

REFLECTION QUESTIONS

1. Have I been trying to build my business in my own strength?
2. In what ways can I practically include God in my daily business operations?
3. How can my business better reflect His covenant and Kingdom purpose?

PRAYER PROMPT

Heavenly Father, thank You for giving me the power to create wealth and for partnering with me in purpose. I surrender every plan, every goal, and every opportunity to You. Teach me how to steward what You've placed in my hands and to walk in wisdom, diligence, and faith. Let everything I build bring glory to You and establish Your covenant on the earth.

—In Jesus' name, Amen.

SCRIPTURE REFERENCES

> *17 then you say in your heart, 'My power and the might of my hand have gained me this wealth.' 18 "And you shall remember the Lord your God, for it is He who gives you power to get wealth, that He may establish His covenant which He swore to your fathers, as it is this day.*
>
> —DEUTERONOMY 8:17–18

> *8 but because the Lord loves you, and because He would keep the oath which He swore to your fathers, the Lord has brought you out with a mighty hand, and redeemed you from the house of bondage, from the hand of Pharaoh king of Egypt. 9 "Therefore know that the Lord your God, He is God, the faithful God who keeps covenant and mercy for a thousand generations with those who love Him and keep His commandments; 10 and He repays those who hate Him to their face, to destroy them. He will not be slack with him who hates Him; He will repay him to his face. 11 Therefore you shall keep the commandment, the statutes, and the*

judgments which I command you today, to observe them. 12 "Then it shall come to pass, because you listen to these judgments, and keep and do them, that the Lord your God will keep with you the covenant and the mercy which He swore to your fathers.

—Deuteronomy 7:8–12

Beloved, I pray that you may prosper in all things and be in health, just as your soul prospers.

—3 John 1:2

She Means Business Declarations

- I live my life rooted in His Word—my business has Kingdom impact.

- I increase each day in wisdom—my business increases each day in wealth.

- The angels of the Lord go before me to bring things to pass in my life.

- I press toward the mark of my high calling in Christ Jesus and fulfill the assignment on my life.

- My business, my purpose, and my destiny flow seamlessly from spending time in His presence.

SHE HAS A PLAN

And then God answered: 'Write this. Write what you see. Write it out in big block letters so that it can be read on the run. This vision-message is a witness pointing to what's coming. It aches for the coming—it can hardly wait! And it doesn't lie. If it seems slow in coming, wait. It's on its way. It will come at the right time.

—HABAKKUK 2:2–3 (MSG)

DEVOTIONAL

Every God-given dream—whether a business, ministry, or church plant—begins with a vision: a divine picture painted in your spirit of what could be through the gifts and talents God has placed within you to pour out through your hands and feet.

In Habakkuk 2, God instructs the prophet to *write the vision*—not think it, wish it, or hide it—*but to make it visible, readable, and clear*. Why? Because your written vision becomes the bridge between faith and manifestation.

As a woman in business, you are called to build what Heaven has already spoken. Yet often, the vision stirring in your heart feels too small—too insignificant to act on. You tell yourself it's not the right time, or that you're not qualified enough. But the truth is, your dream isn't dying from lack of opportunity—*it's being smothered by fear.*

Fear of *failure.*
Fear of *what others will think.*
Fear that *you're not good enough.*

But God says the first step toward seeing your vision fulfilled is simple: *write it down.*

> *Write it out in big block letters so that it can be read on the run.*
>
> —Habakkuk 2:2 (MSG)

Who needs to read it? *You do!* And those God will send to help you do it.

Put your vision where you can see it—on your bathroom mirror, car visor, or workspace—so it stays before your eyes as you run your race.

As a lifelong graphic designer, every time I start a new business, I begin with what God has placed in my heart. I write the mission and vision first, then bring it to life visually through design. That's how I see what God is showing me.

Maybe you're an illustrator—*paint it.*
A poet—*write about it.*
A videographer—*film it.*
A builder—*sketch it out.*

Whatever your gift, use it to express the vision. Write what you see and make it plain so that when others read it, they immediately understand what God has placed in your heart.

That's how you take the first step toward fulfilling the vision, the call, and the purpose God has placed you on this earth to do.

Your only assignment right now? *Write it down and make it plain.*

Then, watch what happens next. A door will open that you didn't see before. You'll meet someone with the resources you need. A book, video, or divine connection will cross your path at just the right time. God will order your steps once you take the first one.

Stay alert. Don't ignore those moments. Don't let doubt, fear, or outside voices talk you out of what the Lord is leading you into. Circumstances will shout, *"You can't do this."* Your insecurities will whisper, *"You're not ready."* Fear will try to paralyze you.

When that happens—*speak the Word*.

> *For God hath not given us the spirit of fear; but of power, and of love, and of a sound mind.*
>
> —2 Timothy 1:7

David did this when he faced Goliath.
Paul and Silas did it when they worshiped in chains.
The woman at the well did it when Jesus met her in her brokenness.

Author and pastor Mark Batterson once said,

> *"The greatest regret at the end of your life will be the lions you didn't chase."*

So chase the lion. Write the vision. Take the first step.

Writing your vision isn't just a business exercise—it's a spiritual act of obedience that moves Heaven and Earth on your behalf! When you write what God says, you anchor Heaven's blueprint to Earth.

Your written vision becomes a prophetic declaration of what will surely come—and it will come right on time.

"Your written vision is the bridge between faith and manifestation."

—Dr. Margo Bush

Faith Action

Set aside 30 minutes today to write out your business or ministry vision in clear, bold, and simple words—big block letters that speak life every time you see them.

Include these key questions to bring clarity and focus:

- What are you building? *(Define your dream.)*

- When will you begin? *(Remember, a dream without a start date is just a wish.)*

- Why are you called to this work? *(Clarify your impact and purpose.)*

- Who are you called to serve? *(Identify the people God has placed on your heart.)*

- Where will you build it? *(Online? Locally? Nationally? Globally?)*

When you're finished, post your written vision somewhere you'll see it daily—your office wall, journal, or bathroom mirror—and let it remind you that every great move of God begins with a written step of faith.

Reflection Questions

1. Have I clearly written down what is in my heart about my business or calling?

2. Where am I struggling to wait on God's timing, and how can I strengthen my faith or my natural skills in the waiting?

3. What practical steps can I take this week to align my actions with the vision God has given me?

4. Who can I share my written vision with for prayer and accountability?

PRAYER PROMPT

Father, thank You for giving me a vision that is rooted in purpose. I will write what I see in my heart because my life is led by You. I will walk in faith and clarity, knowing that I am well able to accomplish all things because greater is He that is in me than He that is in the world. I am strong in the Lord, and I can do all things through Christ who strengthens me. I was born for greatness, and I work like it depends on me, and trust You like it all depends on You. I am confident that You are working behind the scenes to fulfill the vision. My business will bring glory to You. What You've spoken over me and to me will come to pass.

—In Jesus' name, Amen.

SCRIPTURE REFERENCES

> *And the Lord answered me, and said, Write the vision, and make it plain upon tables....*
>
> —Habakkuk 2:2–3 (KJV)

> Then the Lord answered me and said, 'Write the vision and engrave it plainly on tablets…'
>
> —Habakkuk 2:2–3 (AMP)

> Then the Lord said to me, 'Write my answer plainly on tablets…'
>
> —Habakkuk 2:2–3 (NLT)

SHE MEANS BUSINESS DECLARATIONS

- I am faithful to write the vision God has placed in my heart.

- I steward it with faith, diligence, and courage.

- Every day, I take steps to begin my God-given assignment, and Heaven aligns with my purpose.

- I am a woman of action, obedience, and relentless diligence.

SHE INCREASES

Increase is coming, so enlarge your tent and add extensions to your dwelling. Hold nothing back! Make the tent ropes longer and the pegs stronger.

—Isaiah 54:2 (TPT)

DEVOTIONAL

Successful businesswomen prepare for growth. Even Jesus did—He did a lot of marketing before He launched His ministry. It takes faith, vision, and preparation to see increase. If you want to expand, you must first increase your capacity for growth.

The Message translation says it like this:

> *Clear lots of ground for your tents! Make your tents large. Spread out! Think big! Use plenty of rope, drive the tent pegs deep. You're going to need lots of elbow room for your growing family (customers). You're going to take over whole nations; you're going to resettle abandoned cities. Don't be afraid—you're not going to be embarrassed. Don't hold back—you're not going to come up short.*
>
> —Isaiah 54:2 (MSG)

Isaiah 54:2 lays out the plan because increase is coming—so get ready for it!

How do you grow? How does a business increase? We have a lot of examples in the Bible about increase, and Isaiah 54 is one that gives us a clear plan of action. It's going to take some faith and courage on your part. Don't wait for your organization to grow and then expand—that will never happen. Get ready, get prepared, get things in order—*then increase will come*.

Isaiah instructs us on how to create increase in four steps:

1. *Enlarge your tent*: make yourself ready for more—where you are and what you're doing.

2. *Add extensions*: make your place bigger and add more services.

3. *Hold nothing back*: don't plan for just a few.

4. *Make the tent ropes longer and the pegs stronger*: prepare and have a strategy because you're going to need to know what to do with all that is coming to you.

What if I fail? What if I don't do it right? What if I don't have enough experience or education? Starting, growing, or expanding a business requires faith, courage, and wisdom. Building a business—even in small steps—requires believing in yourself and the courage to act on that belief.

> *I can do all things through Christ, which strengtheneth me.*
>
> —Philippians 4:13

> *I know what it means to lack, and I know what it means to experience overwhelming abundance. For I'm trained in the secret of overcoming all things, whether in fullness or in hunger. And I find that the strength of Christ's explosive power infuses me to conquer every difficulty.*
>
> —Philippians 4:12–13 (TPT)

Each time I started a business or wanted to expand the one I had, it came with a huge amount of fear and self-doubt—the kind of fear that made me break out in sweats at night. Each time I felt like Jonah, shut up in the belly of a whale. Each time I had to overcome fear, uncertainty, and the *"what ifs."* But on the other side of fear is opportunity, and on the other side of self-doubt is prosperity. That's why God is leading you there. (See John 16:13)

Many times, we are praying for growth—to make more money or increase our revenue—but we don't like what it looks like to get there. *"Go to the ant, thou sluggard; consider her ways, and be wise."* — Proverbs 6:6 You may have to market more, make more sales calls, schedule more interviews, or hire more people.

Sometimes we have the misconception that if we just open the doors or put up the website, customers will start flooding in. Much like the 1989 movie *Field of Dreams*, the phrase *"If you build it, they will come"* became a popular catchphrase. I have to admit, I might have thought the same thing—I might have believed too, like so many, if I open the doors, the customers will pour in. When few came, I realized there was more to growing an organization than opening the doors, providing a service, building a website, or just praying hard. Don't get me wrong—I believe in praying hard. But I know, like author and speaker Mark Batterson puts it: *"I work like it depends on me, and pray like it depends on God."*

You will have to have a lot of courage, believe in yourself and act on that belief. You might even have to do what I did—put sticky notes all over the house including my bathroom mirror to remind myself what the Word says about ME. Stop listening to that inner voice of self-doubt—

speak to yourself until breakthrough comes. You will have to say it, speak it, and sing it until that wall of fear falls down. Because on the other side of fear, there is wealth and prosperity.

Jabez prayed, *"Bless me indeed, and enlarge my territory."* Are you praying that but haven't seen it manifest? There are requirements for anyone desiring to succeed.

First, reject smallness. Enlargement requires stepping out of small boxes, small routines, small thinking, and a limited view of wealth building. Bottom line—*you must reject a lack mentality!* Caleb and Joshua saw a place of opportunity, but the rest shrank back and remained small. Caleb and Joshua believed it could be done; the others were afraid to try and stayed small-minded.

A colleague once said to me, *"$2 million is nothing."* I said, *"Okay."* He replied, *"No! No! I mean I want you to really see that $2 million is nothing."* I actually think the Lord was speaking to me at that very moment to enlarge my thinking. I've never looked back!

Second, enlarging your tent means making room for new business, clients, products, services, bigger offices, or even new land. Expansion will require more of you, more of your faith, more of your time, and more believing in yourself. New employees will *s-t-r-e-t-c-h* you! Serving more clients will demand more work, more patience, and deeper reliance on God. If you want more—if you're tired of barely paying bills or struggling to make payroll—God is saying, *"Enlarge and stretch."* You will never see a miracle in your business or finances until you stretch your faith for increase and take the steps to grow.

When God tells you to lengthen your cords, it means expand your reach, widen your marketing, and stretch your sales team. Tents need longer cords to remain secure. And once you lengthen your cords, you must also strengthen your stakes—implement better policies, shore up weak procedures, and deepen your organizational foundations. Building a business is like growing a large tree—*the wider the branches spread, the deeper the roots must grow.*

Then it will require of belief in yourself. No one can give that to you, except you. You're going to feel like you are just *'faking it until you make it.'* I challenge you to look deeper and see it as *faithing* it until you make it!

"It's time to stop playing small. You were created for greatness—and she means business."

—Dr. Margo Bush

Faith Action

1. Find a book, podcast, or speaker you can follow that specializes in growing your belief in you.

2. Take actionable steps this week to speak to that inner voice of self-doubt and conquer it.

3. Speak Isaiah 54:2 over your business each morning: Increase is coming! I hold nothing back. I make my ropes longer and my tent pegs stronger.

Reflection Questions

1. Where have I been limiting my business or myself due to fear or a lack mindset?

2. What steps can I take this week to expand my capacity for increase?

3. How am I using my faith to trust God with the growth He has planned for me?

Prayer Prompt

"Father, thank You for calling me to increase. Help me conquer any self-doubt in me that I need to get rid of. Show me where I am thinking too small and show me how to think bigger. Show me how to expand, grow, and prepare for increase. I thank You for wisdom to strengthen the foundations of my business. Let every step I take be in alignment with Your plan for abundance and prosperity.

In Jesus' name, Amen."

SCRIPTURE REFERENCES

"Increase is coming, so enlarge your tent and add extensions to your dwelling. Hold nothing back! Make the tent ropes longer and the pegs stronger.

—ISAIAH 54:2 (TPT)

The steps of a good man are ordered by the Lord, And He delights in his way.

—PSALM 37:23

And Jabez called on the God of Israel saying, "Oh, that You would bless me indeed, and enlarge my [a]territory, that Your hand would be with me, and that You would keep me from evil, that I may not cause pain!" So God granted him what he requested.

—1 CHRONICLES 4:10 (JABEZ PRAYER)

SHE MEANS BUSINESS DECLARATIONS

- I rid self-doubt and replace it with who He says I am.
- I am the head and not the tail, above and not beneath.
- I can do all things, for greater is He that is in me than He that is in the world.
- I was born for greatness.
- It is no accident that I am here, born at this time, living in this place because Your plans are my plans.
- I receive increase into my business.
- I hold nothing back.

- I stretch my capacity to grow, lengthen my reach, and strengthen my foundations.

- God is my guide, and abundance is my portion.

DAY 4

SHE PROSPERS

> Wise people are builders—they build families, businesses, communities. And through intelligence and insight their enterprises are established and endure.
>
> —PROVERBS 24:3 (TPT)

DEVOTIONAL

I want to be wise, don't you? Proverbs says that as we become filled with Lady Wisdom, we become builders of our families, businesses, churches, and communities. How do I know that? Because Proverbs 24:5 tells us that our enterprises are established and endure.

Throughout the book of Proverbs, Lady Wisdom calls us to esteem her above all else, to make her a priority. Wisdom invites us to receive the best way to live—a more excellent and noble way of living. She offers knowledge and understanding in her hand. When you receive wisdom, you gain guidance on how to build your life God's way.

Proverbs 24:4 says, "And through intelligence and insight their enterprises are established and endure." What a powerful message! Lady Wisdom provides a blueprint for success in building a strong family and an ever-increasing business. Whether you have a family, run a business, or both, Lady Wisdom will guide you through it all.

The entire book of Proverbs is about the art of successful living. Every day, we encounter problems, fears, and challenges. Revelation, knowledge, and practical understanding are wrapped up in the metaphor of Lady Wisdom. She is our guide, a hostess who graciously invites us to come and dine at her table. When you accept her invitation, revelation, knowledge, and understanding are imparted to you through her divine hand.

Moms, wisdom is your answer. You don't have to feel stressed or without direction—Lady Wisdom is your guiding light. If you are called—yes, called—to stay at home and care for a bustling household, Wisdom equips you to build strong children and a thriving home. For moms who work outside the home or run a business, Wisdom teaches you how to balance responsibilities and excel in both your family and career.

> *"You don't have to leave one behind or feel less than if you work in the home or own a business and have a family. You are called to the place where you serve."*
>
> —Dr. Margo Bush

Wisdom will teach you how to build when you hunger after her. Lady Wisdom wants to be a part of your life. Love her, pursue her, and chase her hard. There are two kinds of builders in this world: the wise and righteous, and the wicked fools. The wise builder possesses revelation, knowledge, and understanding. A wise builder is a God-lover, a wisdom chaser, a destiny dreamer.

Philippians 4:13 says, "I can do all things through Christ who strengthens me." I love The Passion Translation of this verse: "For I'm trained in the secret of overcoming all things, whether in fullness or in hunger. And I find that the strength of Christ's explosive power infuses me to conquer every difficulty." I want to be trained in that secret of overcoming all things—don't you? Lady Wisdom reaches out her hand and invites us into that secret place.

Running a household and a business isn't easy, but His explosive power infuses you to face every challenge as you accept Lady Wisdom's invitation.

Let's look more closely at wisdom's instructions in Proverbs 24:4:

Intelligence—the ability to acquire and apply knowledge and skills.

Insight—the capacity to gain a deep, instinctive understanding.

Whether your "enterprise" is your home, your business, or both, applying revelation, knowledge, skillful guidance, and insight will teach you how to build something worthy of a legacy. When we invite Lady Wisdom and the ways of God into our planning, our families grow stronger, our businesses stand firm, and our communities thrive.

Dine at Lady Wisdom's table as much as you can, because uncommon wisdom will lead you into uncommon success.

"Uncommon wisdom will lead you into uncommon success."

—Dr. Margo Bush

Faith Action

Today, ask for wisdom that will lead to prosperity in one area of your business or home—and follow it.

Write down a decision or challenge you face and ask and seek the wisdom of God to guide you.

Take one actionable step for 31 days that reflects His guidance and practical wisdom.

Reflection Questions

1. Where in my life or business do I need wisdom to build stronger foundations?

2. Am I seeking wisdom daily, or relying on my own understanding?

3. How can I apply insight and intelligence to increase my influence and impact?

Prayer Prompt

"Father, I ask for Your wisdom and insight today. Guide my decisions, bless my work, and help me build my home, business, and relationships according to Your plan. Let Your wisdom lead me into success and prosperity for Your Kingdom.

In Jesus' name, Amen."

Scripture References

Wise people are builders—they build families, businesses, communities. And through intelligence and insight their enterprises are established and endure. [4] Because of their skilled leadership, the hearts of people are filled with the treasures of wisdom and the pleasures of spiritual wealth.

—Proverbs 24:3–4 (TPT)

Wisdom can make anyone into a mighty warrior, and revelation-knowledge increases strength.

—Proverbs 24:5 (TPT)

I know what it means to lack, and I know what it means to experience overwhelming abundance. For I'm trained in the secret of overcoming all things, whether in fullness or in hunger. And I find that the strength of Christ's explosive power infuses me to conquer every difficulty.

—Philippians 4:13 (TPT)

I can do all things through Christ who strengthens me.

—Philippians 4:13 (KJV)

SHE MEANS BUSINESS DECLARATION

- I walk in wisdom, insight, and understanding.

- I am a builder of lasting success and Kingdom impact because I have a covenant with the Almighty.

- I am a creator of successful businesses.

- My decisions are guided by faith and prosperity principles, and my business, home, and life flourish under divine direction.

DAY 5

SHE FINDS FAVOR

And Ruth the Moabitess said unto Naomi, Let me now go to the field, and glean ears of corn after him in whose sight I shall find grace. And she said unto her, Go, my daughter.

—RUTH 2:2 (KJV)

DEVOTIONAL

The Hebrew word for guardian-redeemer is a legal term meaning one who has the obligation to redeem a relative in serious difficulty. Ruth needed a redeemer, and so did we. Sin left us in desperate need of redemption, and just as Boaz stepped in for Ruth, Jesus stepped in for us. He is our ultimate Guardian-Redeemer—the One who continually brings us back, restores what's been lost, and positions us for divine favor.

But notice something powerful in Ruth's story—she didn't sit back in sorrow, waiting for her circumstances to change. She didn't complain about her loss, her lack, or the impossibility of her situation. Instead, her faith became her fuel, and wisdom became her plan.

Ruth said, "...in whose sight I shall find grace" (Ruth 2:2). The NIV says, "in whose eyes I find favor." Webster defines grace as unmerited divine assistance, mercy, pardon, a special favor or privilege. That's exactly what we carry as Kingdom women in business—special favor when we walk into boardrooms, make presentations, submit proposals, or pitch ideas. Grace is our business advantage. Divine assistance goes before us when we're negotiating a contract, launching a startup, or expanding a vision.

But Ruth didn't just speak faith—she put her faith to work. Ruth 2:7 says, "She came into the field and has remained here from morning till now, except for a short rest." She got up early. She showed up. She stayed the course. Her diligence preceded her favor.

That's the posture of a woman who means business—spiritually, financially, and purposefully. She didn't wait for provision; she positioned herself for it. She didn't hope someone would notice her worth; she demonstrated it through her work.

When I became a young widow, I had to make the same hard decision. I remember the days when grief could have easily paralyzed me—when it would have been easier to retreat and stop moving forward. But like Ruth, I chose to go to the field. I chose to put my hand to what God had placed in my house (See 2 Kings 4). I showed up, stood up, and put my makeup on every day, even when my heart was broken, when my grief was so deep that I could hardly breathe. And God met me in the middle of my diligence.

That's what faith and prosperity look like in real life—not just abundance in your bank account (that will come), but abundance in your belief, in your work ethic, and in your expectation that God will favor your field.

Ruth found favor among workers, leaders, and eventually with Boaz. Why? Because she carried herself with humility, excellence, and unwavering faith. Everyone who watched her work respected her. She wasn't defined by her widowhood—she was defined by her faith and courage.

And that's what She Means Business is all about. It's about a woman who refuses to give up, who dares to believe that favor will meet her for her future, who understands that prosperity is not a one-time miracle but the fruit of consistent, faith-filled pursuit of her passion to prosper and create Kingdom impact.

So today, I ask you:

- Do you have the kind of faith that finds favor among your staff, colleagues, and peers?
- Do you show up early to glean in the field God has assigned you?
- Do you trust that favor goes before you—in every client call, every business meeting, every marketing effort, every proposal?

Because when a woman of faith gets up, shows up, and goes to work, she can expect God's favor—heaven takes notice.

"Faith is your fuel, the Word is your weapon, and every setback becomes a setup for your next comeback."

—Dr. Margo Bush

Faith Action

Go to work on what God has placed in your hands today. Show up early, stay the course, and do your work with excellence.

Speak this declaration:

"I operate in divine favor today. Every effort I make, every call I place, every meeting I attend is met with God's grace and opens doors for Kingdom impact."

Reflection Questions

1. How can I position myself to receive favor in my work today?

2. Am I consistently showing up and putting in the effort God has entrusted to me?

3. Where am I waiting for provision instead of stepping into what God has already given me?

PRAYER PROMPT

"Father, thank You for Your favor that goes before me. Teach me to stay diligent and faithful in my work, to trust Your timing, and to walk in the opportunities You have placed before me. Let my faith produce favor that impacts my business, my family, and my community.

In Jesus' name, Amen."

SCRIPTURE REFERENCES

And Ruth the Moabitess said unto Naomi, Let me now go to the field, and glean ears of corn after him in whose sight I shall find grace. And she said unto her, Go, my daughter.

–RUTH 2:2 (KJV)

And Ruth said to Naomi, 'Let me go to the fields and pick up the leftover grain behind anyone in whose eyes I find favor.' Naomi said to her, "Go ahead, my daughter.

–RUTH 2:2 (NIV)

SHE MEANS BUSINESS DECLARATION

- I step into my God-given assignment with diligence, faith, and excellence.

- Favor surrounds every decision I make, every relationship I build, and every opportunity I pursue.

- I am a woman who means business, and my work produces Kingdom impact.

- Favor is upon me, and my diligence and faith in private pay off when I meet opportunity.

DAY 6

SHE WAITS UPON HIM

> At each and every sunrise you will hear my voice as I prepare my sacrifice of prayer to you. Every morning I lay out the pieces of my life on the altar and wait for your fire to fall upon my heart.
>
> —PSALM 5:3 (TPT)

DEVOTIONAL

Every successful Kingdom business, every Kingdom-minded entrepreneur begins not in a boardroom, but at the altar. This passage paints a powerful image of surrender and partnership with God—"I lay out the pieces of my life on the altar and wait for Your fire to fall upon my heart."

Your altar is where vision, strategy, and prayer meet. It's where your plans are refined, your motives are purified, and your heart aligns with Heaven's agenda. Each morning, you have an appointment with the Creator of the Universe, the Son of the Most High, the Bright and Morning Star, and Miracle Worker to offer a heart full of gratitude and worship. You have an open invitation with the greatest business partner

and divine leader of your life to present your business, goals, and challenges before Him—inviting the Lord to breathe His wisdom, direction, and favor over every piece.

When you begin your day with this level of spiritual surrender, you move from striving to flowing, from frustration to supernatural success, and from trouble into triumph. God leads you not just in spiritual matters, but in business strategy, decision-making, and innovation. Your prayer becomes a divine exchange—your plans for His power, your uncertainty for His clarity, your limitations for His limitless ability.

When you make your prayer life your business strategy, you invite supernatural results. When you make His Word a priority, you can confidently say, "Your Word have I hid in my heart that I might not sin against you." The altar becomes your boardroom. The Holy Spirit becomes your Chief Advisor. Every decision becomes an act of faith that advances God's Kingdom through your work.

It takes practice to establish the habit of preparing a time to meet Him in prayer, just like you would prepare for a board meeting. The Hebrew word for "prepare" in Psalms 5:3 is 'arak'—a priestly term meaning to light the altar fire, prepare a sacrifice, and lay it in order upon the altar to be consumed. The Aramaic text states, "At dawn I shall be ready and shall appear before you." The Hebrew can also be translated, "I'll be on the watchtower [for the answer to come]."

There is a pattern we see in Psalms 5:3:

1. **Rise up before dawn and be ready.**

2. **Appear before Him with a voice of gratitude.** Let the first thing your King and God hears be thankfulness—enter His gates with thanksgiving.

3. **Prepare your requests in order.** Plan ahead so you can lay out your requests like a business agenda.

Wait in worship for the answer.

Lay your requests before Him as you would with a business partner. What are the next steps for your company? What challenges need addressing? What strategies should you discuss with your Divine

Partner? Prepare your agenda, lay out your requests in order, and bring them to the altar to hear His direction.

"Your altar is your boardroom, and the Holy Spirit is your Chief Advisor—when you seek Him first success will come."

—Dr. Margo Bush

Faith Action

1. Take 10–15 minutes each morning this week to "lay out the pieces" of your business before God—your goals, finances, clients, and upcoming decisions.

2. Speak these daily confessions of faith and surrender your will to His:

   - I lay out the pieces of my life and my business on the altar of God.

   - The Lord leads me in every decision and directs my path with peace.

   - God's fire falls upon my plans, purifying, empowering, and prospering them.

   - My business is a tool for Kingdom impact.

   - I walk in divine partnership with the Holy Spirit every day.

3. Journal any ideas, or scriptures that come to your heart during prayer. Those are divine strategies for your next level of success.

Reflection Questions

1. Am I beginning my day with the Lord before I begin my work?

2. How can I make my business decisions a form of worship and obedience?

3. What requests or challenges do I need to lay before God today with clarity and faith?

PRAYER PROMPT

"Father, I commit this day, my business, and my vision to You. Teach me to wait upon You, listen to Your voice, and follow Your direction. Let Your favor and wisdom guide every decision I make, and may my business bring glory to Your Kingdom.

In Jesus' name, Amen."

SCRIPTURE REFERENCES

My voice shalt thou hear in the morning, O LORD; in the morning will I direct my prayer unto thee, and will look up.

—P<small>SALM</small> 5:3 (KJV)

At each and every sunrise you will hear my voice as I prepare my sacrifice of prayer to you. Every morning I lay out the pieces of my life on the altar and wait for your fire to fall upon my heart."

—P<small>SALMS</small> 5:3 (TPT)

SHE MEANS BUSINESS DECLARATION

- I begin each day seeking the Lord first as my business partner.

- I rise early, prepare my requests, and wait in faith for His direction.

- Every step I take today is led by His wisdom, favor, and power.

- I will wait on Him in prayer and praise—the answer will come, the victory will come, direction will come.

SHE WALKS IN WISDOM

> Wisdom extends to you long life in one hand, and wealth and promotion in the other. Out of her mouth flow righteousness, and her words release both law and mercy.
>
> —Proverbs 3:16 (TPT)

Devotional

Proverbs declares loud and clear that wisdom is the principal thing—get all you can (Proverbs 4:7). Wisdom is more than information; it is the divine ability to align your words, decisions, and actions with God's heart. When a woman walks in wisdom, she carries Heaven's blueprint for success.

Proverbs 3:16 paints a beautiful picture of what wisdom offers: in one hand, long life—divine health, endurance, and peace—and the other, wealth and promotion. That means wisdom doesn't just lengthen your years; it increases your prosperity and influence.

Promotion flows from wisdom because she teaches us to handle what we have with stewardship, strategy, and spiritual sensitivity. True wealth is more than money—it's the capacity to multiply resources, opportunities, and people. It's the ability to create value that benefits others and glorifies God. Promotion comes when wisdom positions you before the right people, at the right time, with the right words.

Wisdom will teach you when to speak and when to stay silent, when to sow and when to save, when to build and when to break away. She's not loud or boastful—she's strategic, precise, and full of peace.

For the woman in business, this truth is transformative. Every decision, every contract, every team meeting becomes an opportunity to release God's wisdom. When you lead with wisdom, your influence increases naturally. You don't have to strive for success—wisdom attracts it.

Your words carry authority. Out of your mouth flows righteousness—speaking what is right—and mercy—balancing truth with compassion. The combination of both releases favor and builds trust, which are the keys to long-term wealth and lasting promotion.

When your business is built on wisdom, you won't chase opportunities; they'll find you. Wisdom stabilizes what hard work alone cannot sustain. Success doesn't always come quickly—so speak carefully, speak truthfully, speak blessings. And remember—wisdom has both hands extended toward you: one filled with long life, and the other with wealth and prosperity. Take both, and build with grace.

"When you walk in wisdom—you carry heaven's blueprint for success."

—Dr. Margo Bush

Faith Action

Invite the Holy Spirit into your business decisions to be your Chief Advisor. Ask Him for divine strategies to grow, promote, and sustain your business.

Take 5 minutes each day to speak over your business and life these declarations:

- I declare blessings over my business, my team, clients, and operations.
- I speak wisdom into every area that needs guidance and growth.
- I confess that wealth, promotion, and divine favor flow today over me because I align my words with God's Word.

Reflection Questions

1. What does wisdom look like in my daily business decisions?
2. Am I building from a place of peace or pressure?
3. How can I invite God's wisdom into my words, leadership, and influence this week?

Prayer Prompt

Lord, I ask for Your wisdom to guide every area of my life and business. Teach me to speak with righteousness and mercy, to lead with peace and discernment, and to walk in alignment with Your heart. I receive both long life and promotion from Your hand.

In Jesus' name, Amen.

Scripture References

Wisdom extends to you long life in one hand, and wealth and promotion in the other. Out of her mouth flow righteousness, and her words release both law and mercy.

—Proverbs 3:16 (TPT)

Wisdom is the principal thing; therefore get wisdom: and with all thy getting get understanding.

—Proverbs 4:7 (KJV)

If any of you lacks wisdom, you should ask God, who gives generously to all without finding fault, and it will be given to you.

—James 1:5 (NIV)

She Means Business Declaration

- As a Kingdom-minded businesswoman I walk in His divine wisdom because I seek Him first.

- I build my business with wisdom, I lead with discernment, and my lips speak with grace.

- Opportunities find me, favor surrounds me, and success follows me.

- I don't strive—I thrive, because I began my day in His presence before I met the world.

- The world is waiting for me—I was born to do great things.

She's a Million Dollar Mom

So Elisha said to her, 'What shall I do for you? Tell me, what do you have in the house?'

And she said, 'Your maidservant has nothing in the house but a jar of oil.

—2 Kings 4:2 (NKJV)

Devotional

This story is one of the most powerful business lessons in Scripture. It begins with a woman in crisis — widowed, in debt, and facing the loss of her sons. I think I love this story so much because it was **my story**. At the age of forty-nine, my husband moved to Heaven very unexpectedly. We had children, a life filled with purpose, and a bright future ahead.

I share a portion of my personal story in Dream Big, Live Big! by Margo Bush (available on Amazon, Bushpublishing.com and everywhere books are sold).

Within this widow woman's home was the very thing God would use to bring her deliverance, wealth, and prosperity—**a single pot of oil.**

Elisha didn't hand her money or pity. He gave her a strategy. God will always give you a divine plan before He gives you a financial breakthrough. The question He still asks today is:

"What do you have in your house?"

For the woman entrepreneur, this story reveals that your miracle is often hidden in what you already possess.

You may have an idea, a skill, a creation, a connection, or a product that seems small—but in God's hands, it's the **seed of overflow.**

Her obedience to follow divine instruction unlocked multiplication. She didn't wait for perfect conditions; she acted on faith.

Notice the Pattern:

- The Lord provided the seed.
- She assessed what she had.
- She followed divine strategy—borrow vessels.
- She shut the door—focusing on her assignment, not the opinions of others.
- She poured out until there were no more vessels.

The oil flowed in proportion to her capacity. When there were no more vessels—no more capacity—the Lord gave her the next step.

That's a business principle: **God will fill the space you make room for.**

Finally, the prophet said, *"Go, sell the oil, pay your debt, and live on the rest."*

Her faith turned into a business—*The Oil Business.*

She moved from **poverty to profit**, from **desperation to destiny**. Notice that it wasn't until she was obedient to take the first step that she received the next step from the prophet.

> *"The steps of a good man (woman) are ordered by the Lord: and he (she) delighteth in His way."*
>
> —Psalm 37:23 (KJV)

> *"Stalwart walks in step with God; his (her) path blazed by God, he's (she's) happy. If he (she) stumbles, he's (she's) not down for long; God has a grip on his (her) hand."*
>
> —Psalm 37:23 (MSG)

Your "oil" is what God has gifted you to do. It might be your voice, your creativity, your writing, your singing, your networking, your coaching, your preaching, your ability to organize, write code, or develop software.

Whatever it is, **God will multiply what you pour in obedience to use what He has gifted you with.**

The miracle is not in waiting for resources—it's in using what you already have. You don't have to wait on Him—He is waiting for you.

Walk in the...

    Power—authority and influence.

    Persistence—perseverance and determination.

    Potential—growth and untapped opportunities.

> *"God will give you a divine plan before He gives you a financial breakthrough."*
>
> —Dr. Margo Bush

FAITH ACTION

- Identify one resource, skill, or connection you already possess that God could multiply in your business.

- Take one practical step today to put that resource into action—even if it feels small.

- Trust God to multiply it beyond what you can see.

REFLECTION QUESTIONS

1. What is the "oil" in your hands that God is asking you to pour out?

2. How can you create space (capacity) for God to increase what you already have?

3. Are there areas where fear or waiting has kept you from taking the first step?

PRAYER PROMPT

"Lord, show me what I already have that You want to multiply. Give me the faith to act, the obedience to follow Your plan, and the courage to pour out what You've placed in my hands. Multiply my efforts for Your glory, and help me steward the overflow wisely.

In Jesus' name, Amen."

SCRIPTURE REFERENCES

A certain woman of the wives of the sons of the prophets cried out to Elisha, saying, "Your servant my husband is dead, and you know that your servant feared the Lord. And the creditor is coming to take my two sons to be his slaves." 2 So Elisha said to her, "What shall I do for you? Tell me, what do you have in the house?" And she said, "Your maidservant has nothing in the house but a jar of oil." 3 Then he said, "Go, borrow vessels from everywhere, from all your neighbors—empty vessels; do not gather just a few.

4 And when you have come in, you shall shut the door behind you and your sons; then pour it into all those vessels, and set aside the full ones." 5 So she went from him and shut the door behind her and her sons, who brought the vessels to her; and she poured it out. 6 Now it came to pass, when the vessels were full, that she said to her son, "Bring me another vessel." And he said to her, "There is not another vessel." So the oil ceased. 7 Then she came and told the man of God. And he said, "Go, sell the oil and pay your debt; and you and your sons live on the rest."

—2 Kings 4:1–7 (NKJV)

The steps of a good man are ordered by the Lord: and he delighteth in his way.

—Psalm 37:23 (KJV)

Stalwart walks in step with God; his path blazed by God he's happy. If he stumbles, he's not down for long; God has a grip on his hand.

—Psalm 37:23(MSG)

She Means Business Declaration

- I am a businesswoman full of wisdom and I walk in prosperity.

- I take what God has placed in my hands and use it to earn more and create financial security.

- I work like it all depends on me, and use my faith to believe like it all depends on Him.

- I have the power within me to multiply my efforts, expand my capacity, and turn my resources into Kingdom impact.

- Today, I step into my destiny as a Million Dollar Mom with purpose, passion, potential, and power.

DAY 9

SHE IS DILIGENT

[6] When you're feeling lazy, come and learn a lesson from this tale of the tiny ant. Yes, all you lazybones, come learn from the example of the ant and enter into wisdom. [7] The ants have no chief, no boss, no manager—no one has to tell them what to do.

—PROVERBS 6:6-7 (TPT)

DEVOTIONAL

In the fast-paced world of business, creativity and vision often get celebrated, but God honors diligence. Proverbs reminds us that success is born not only from big ideas, but from consistent discipline, preparation, and faithful action.

The ant doesn't wait for motivation; it moves in wisdom. It doesn't need supervision or applause to stay productive. Its diligence today secures its future tomorrow.

Proverbs 6:6-11 is worth reading once a month to remind us that success will not happen if it is not met with diligence. It is so clear in the Passion Translation what is expected to be rich and not fall into poverty.

> *6When you're feeling lazy, come and learn a lesson from this tale of the tiny ant. Yes, all you lazybones, come learn from the example of the ant and enter into wisdom. 7The ants have no chief, no boss, no manager—no one has to tell them what to do. 8You'll see them working and toiling all summer long, stockpiling their food in preparation for winter. 9So wake up, sleepyhead. How long will you lie there? When will you wake up and get out of bed? 10If you keep nodding off and thinking, "I'll do it later," or say to yourself, "I'll just sit back awhile and take it easy," just watch how the future unfolds! 11By making excuses you'll learn what it means to go without. Poverty will pounce on you like a bandit and move in as your roommate for life."*

—PROVERBS 6:6-11

For women in business, this is a divine reminder: your preparation in private determines your promotion in public. It's not just about working hard—it's about working faithfully, even when no one is watching. Procrastination may feel harmless in the moment, but it quietly steals potential, opportunity, and momentum. Every "I'll do it later" can cost you time, influence, or revenue that God intended to multiply.

Jesus illustrated diligence in the Parable of the Talents (Matthew 25:14-30). A master entrusted his servants with resources while he traveled. Two of the servants invested and multiplied what they were given; the third buried his talent out of fear. When the master returned, he rewarded those who acted faithfully and wisely, but rebuked the servant who did nothing. The lesson is clear: God honors action, effort, and wise stewardship. In business, diligence—consistent work, faithful investment of time, and strategic planning—leads to growth and blessing. Waiting for perfect conditions or avoiding effort out of fear results in missed opportunities.

James 2:17 reminds us, *"Faith by itself, if it is not accompanied by action, is dead."* Your vision, ideas, and dreams are important, but they must be paired with daily action. Showing up, putting in the work, and being consistent—even when it's challenging—activates God's favor and multiplies your results.

Diligence in business is also about preparation and attention to detail. The Proverbs ant doesn't leave food to chance; she anticipates the future and plans for it. Likewise, a diligent businesswoman builds systems, tracks finances, invests in learning, and plans ahead. She doesn't allow complacency or procrastination to determine her outcomes. Every task done faithfully, no matter how small, lays the foundation for long-term growth.

Let me share a story from my own experience: When I first took over our book publishing company, I had no idea how to grow a business. But I committed to showing up every day, learning every process, and being faithful in small tasks—sorting inventory, learning contracts, handling customer calls. The consistency of those actions built momentum. Within months, the business began to flourish, and within two years, we had expanded operations and cleared significant debt. Diligence turns seemingly ordinary actions into extraordinary results.

So, take note: the path to success is rarely sudden. It is built brick by brick, hour by hour, task by task. Faith without action is dead, and talent without diligence never reaches its full potential.

Key Principles of Diligence in Business:

- Show up consistently, even when motivation wanes.

- Plan ahead and anticipate challenges.

- Invest your time, talents, and resources on what produces business growth.

- Take action on the opportunities God places in your hands—don't wait around.

- Do not fear failure—learning is part of the process.

- Trust God to multiply your diligent efforts.

When you adopt a spirit of diligence, poverty cannot overtake you. Faithful effort becomes a magnet for opportunity, divine connections, and breakthrough. Be like the ant, the wise servant, and the faithful entrepreneur—consistent, prepared, and committed to the work God has entrusted to you.

"Success doesn't wait for motivation; it moves with wisdom."

—Dr. Margo Bush

Faith Action

- Model the ant: Each morning, set three intentional, productive goals and commit to completing them before the day ends.

- Eliminate excuses: Replace "I'll do it later" with "I'll do it now." Every small act of obedience and consistency builds lasting success.

- Prepare in advance: Use your weekends or the one hour before bedtime to plan for the next day and week ahead—business strategies, scheduling appointments, workout times, place and time for spirit-led meditation and meetings that will move your business forward.

Reflection Questions

1. Where in my business am I procrastinating or waiting for the "perfect time"?

2. What daily habits can I implement to ensure consistent progress?

3. How does my faith guide me to take action instead of remaining idle?

Prayer Prompt

"Father, help me to be diligent in the actions I need to take each day in my business to see success. Help me to be faithful in the small things, disciplined in my work, and consistent in my efforts. Teach me how to boldly take the steps You have placed before me today and trust that

You will multiply my actions. I lay aside fear, laziness, and excuses and replace them with faith, and diligence.

In Jesus' name, Amen."

SCRIPTURE REFERENCES

Faith by itself, if it is not accompanied by action, is dead.

—JAMES 2:17 (NIV)

The servants who diligently invested and multiplied what they were given were rewarded, while the one who buried his mina out of fear was rebuked.

—LUKE 19:12-17 (PARABLE OF THE TEN MINAS)

SHE MEANS BUSINESS DECLARATION

- I commit to being diligent in the area of my business that needs attention.

- I will show up, grow up and step up to act consistently on the vision God has placed in me.

- Today, not tomorrow, but today I will steward my time, talents, and resources wisely.

- I move forward in purpose, power, and persistence.

SHE BUYS A FIELD

She sets her heart upon a field and takes it as her own. She labors there to plant the living vines.

—Proverbs 31:16 (TPT)

DEVOTIONAL

Proverbs 31:16 paints a picture of a woman full of courage, faith, and fruitfulness, with strategic vision and diligence. The word translated "field" here means land or country, showing that her vision is large. Sometimes the dreams you have seem too big—bigger than what you think you can do. They might feel challenging or even intimidating. If your dream doesn't scare you, it's not big enough.

This woman understood a critical principle: anything God calls you to do is usually bigger than you can accomplish on your own. That's how you know it's from Him—it will require faith and dependency upon the Master. Without Him, even the best plans and intentions fall short. But with Him, the vision is achievable, fruitful, and aligned with His Kingdom purposes for your life.

"By the fruit of her hands, she plants a vineyard"—her labor was not aimless. She was intentional, purposeful, and passionate about producing results, both naturally and spiritually. She understood that success is measured not only in profits but in the people her work impacts—customers, employees, partners, and community. Every action, every decision, every conversation was an investment in the fruit of her labor.

Your business is your vineyard. The relationships you build, the services you provide, the people you hire and influence—these are the living vines that grow and multiply under your stewardship. She steps into abundance because she has been skillful, invests diligently, and partners with God to learn Kingdom business so she will produce fruit that lasts.

God is calling you to set your heart on your field. What is it that God is calling you to do? Does it seem too big for you to build or accomplish on your own? Identify the big, God-sized dream He has assigned to you. It's time to take ownership, to use your faith, and step into it. Labor faithfully. The vision is not just for your gain—it's for fruit that produces a harvest in other people's lives and expands His Kingdom.

Tips to step into your God-sized dream:

- Write it down—all of it.

- Craft it into a story that will read well.

- Read it out loud to yourself—let it come alive in you.

- Find someone you can trust (friend, sister, mother, spouse) to read it to.

- Take one action step each day that moves you into your God-given assignment.

We often look at this Proverbs 31 woman as someone impossible to attain—too special, too wonderful, amazingly blessed. In reality, this is exactly what God is speaking over us. He is saying you are a Proverbs 31 woman. You are the bride of Christ. He's calling you out and up to a higher place to do Kingdom business with Him—household business, raising children to walk uprightly before Him, blessed in your marriage because you have spent time cultivating your relationships, walking in wisdom, and not letting your emotions or feelings control your day. We are who He says we are—a Proverbs 31 Woman. Claim it, speak it, and build your faith around it. Let Proverbs 31 be your guiding light to fulfilling your God-sized dream.

When I was in my twenties and newly married, I had a bad habit of wearing my feelings on my shoulders. So many things my husband said, I took as a personal attack—what I wore, what I cooked, how I cooked. He was a kind and gracious man, but I had a problem with my own self-confidence. As a result, I would end up stomping away to my room like a child until I got over it.

One day, I was alone at home cleaning with the television on, listening to a preacher. I can't remember any other part of the message except one sentence that still rings in my ears today—forty years later. He said, *"If you don't stop wearing your feelings on your shoulders, God will never be able to use you."* From that day forward, I stopped that childish behavior—Glory to God! That is one time it felt as though God delivered me instantly. I walked free and never looked back.

Since then, I've ministered in every state at least once—most states several times, in the US except Alaska and Hawaii—and taught in Bible schools and churches in more than seven countries. I've been part of one of the most impactful children's ministries in my twenties, traveling coast to coast teaching in churches and children's workers conferences. I had a part on a wildly successful children's television show that impacted the world and taught for many years at a Bible College that trained ministers to go out and minister globally. I had the honor to pastor for fifteen years, sending more than sixty students to Bible school to fulfill their own ministry callings.

I'm so glad I obeyed God when I heard that preacher, took control of my feelings, and learned to follow Him. Look what I would have missed. Don't miss your calling in the marketplace or in ministry just because you're too scared to step out or take more territory. Your dream is not too big—it's not big enough. Your vision is not too large—it's not large enough. Your passion to prosper is not too small—it's not enough for all that God wants for you.

From this day forward, don't look at the Proverbs 31 woman as someone you can't attain—but as someone you already are. Speak over yourself who the Word says you are, not how you feel.

Proverbs 31:16–19 (Personalized):

16 "She [your name] sets her heart upon a field and takes it as her own. She [your name] labors there to plant the living vines.

17 She [your name] wraps herself in strength, might, and power in all her works.

18 She [your name] tastes and experiences a better substance, and her shining light will not be extinguished, no matter how dark the night.

19 She [your name] stretches out her hands to help the needy and lays hold of the wheels of government."

This woman is confident, strategic in her life and family goals, and powerful in her community.

"Your dream is not too big—it's not big enough. Your vision is not too large—it's not large enough. Your passion to prosper is not too big—it's not enough big enough for all God has called you to do."

—Dr. Margo Bush

Faith Action

- Identify the God-sized dream He has assigned to you. Write it down in detail.

- Craft it into a story that inspires action and vision.

- Read it aloud to yourself daily, letting it come alive in your heart.

- Share it with a trusted friend, mentor, or family member for accountability.

- Take one actionable step each day to move into your God-given assignment.

REFLECTION QUESTIONS

1. What is the "field" God has placed before you in your life or business?
2. Are you hesitating because the vision feels too big? If so, what step of faith can you take today?
3. How can you invest your time, talent, and resources today to begin cultivating your field?
4. In what ways have you allowed feelings or fear to hold you back, and how can you surrender that to God?

PRAYER PROMPT

"Lord, help me to be courageous to step into the field You've assigned to me. Help me labor faithfully, invest wisely and become all you have called me to become. Help me to partner with You in every decision. Let my actions produce prosperity and provision for my family and my business. Cause my actions to produce fruit that blesses others and expands Your Kingdom. I claim the strength, courage, and provision to fulfill every dream in my heart.

In Jesus' name, Amen."

SCRIPTURE REFERENCES

She sets her heart upon a field and takes it as her own. She labors there to plant the living vines.

—Proverbs 31:16 (TPT)

The steps of a good man are ordered by the LORD: and he delighteth in his way.

—Psalm 37:23 (KJV)

> *Stalwart walks in step with God; his path blazed by God, he's happy. If he stumbles, he's not down for long; God has a grip on his hand.*
>
> —Psalm 37:23 (MSG)

She Means Business Declaration

- I, [your name], set my heart upon the field God has given me and work it in wisdom.

- I am wrapped in strength, might, and power.

- I taste and experience a better life, and my shining light will not be extinguished.

- I am confident, strategic, and powerful.

- I am a woman of might, valor, virtue, wisdom, and strength. I don't give up, I fight for what's right and I stand in the face of the enemy with confidence in my calling.

SHE STEPS INTO OVERFLOW

A slacker will know what it means to be poor, while the hard worker becomes wealthy.

—PROVERBS 10:4 (TPT)

DEVOTIONAL

How does wealth and riches come? And how does poverty creep in? The answer is simple—hard work brings wealth, and laziness invites lack.

Poverty rarely arrives in a rush; it sneaks in through the quiet door of procrastination. It begins with small, subtle thoughts like, "I'll do that later," or "I'll call that client tomorrow." Each delay, each moment of hesitation, slows the momentum that prosperity requires. Let that sink in: prosperity requires staying in motion. Diligence—prompt action—keeps you moving toward increase. Every time you stop, even for a little while, momentum stalls.

The Kingdom of God operates on divine principles, and one of them is reward through diligence. The King James Version says it like this: *"He becometh poor that dealeth with a slack hand: But the hand of the diligent maketh rich."*

When you work with diligence, and take action on what God tells you to do, you position yourself for wealth and abundance. You won't automatically become rich—there are many right steps you must take to create wealth in your business. But when you apply the correct principles and strategies, wealth becomes your friend. Think of it like baking a cake: just putting an egg in the mix doesn't automatically produce a cake. There are other ingredients you must add, but you cannot leave the egg out either.

If we neglect the small things, delay action, or compromise truth, we invite loss. Integrity protects our business and positions us for overflow.

Kingdom-minded women don't neglect the small things, tell a "white lie to get a client to sign on," or delay what we know we should do—we compromise integrity—that's a breeding ground for lack in our business. Integrity is a part of the recipe for those who want to succeed in business. The Word calls this evil behavior, because it leads us away from God's way of doing business.

If you're struggling in your business, take an honest look at your actions. Are you diligent or always delaying? Are you working smart, with integrity, or are you busy worrying instead of building? **Worry is disguised procrastination.** It drains your energy and produces no fruit.

Ruth provides a perfect illustration of diligence, faith, and stepping into overflow. As a widow in a foreign land, she could have chosen despair, complaining, or waiting for someone else to provide for her. Instead, she went to work. Ruth got up early, went to the fields, and gleaned grain diligently from sunrise to sunset. She worked with integrity, humility, and perseverance.

Her hard work positioned her for divine favor. Boaz noticed her diligence, her faithfulness, and eventually she entered into a season of abundance and blessing. Ruth's story demonstrates that the hand of the diligent truly makes rich, and that faithful action opens the door for God's supernatural provision.

Notice the principles Ruth modeled:

She **showed up every day** and stayed consistent.

She **worked faithfully and with integrity**.

She **followed guidance** from Naomi while staying proactive.

She **trusted God's timing** and moved in faith.

Just as Ruth stepped into overflow by acting faithfully, we too must combine our dreams with action. As James 2:17 reminds us: *"Faith by itself, if it is not accompanied by action, is dead."* Your diligence positions you to receive both natural and supernatural increase.

"God will not do for you what He has already told you to do."

—Dr. Margo Bush

Faith Action

Take 30 minutes today to evaluate your daily habits.

- Write down three areas where procrastination or fear has held you back.
- Replace them with decisive, faith-filled action steps.
- Speak this declaration out loud every morning.

Reflection Questions

1. Where have I been delaying action, and how can I change that today?
2. What tasks or projects will require consistent effort over time before I see results?

3. How can I combine diligence, integrity, and faith in my daily business practices?

PRAYER PROMPT

"Lord, teach me to work diligently in every area of my business. Help me to walk with integrity, trust Your timing, and step into overflow. Strengthen my hands and guide my heart as I fulfill the assignment of God on my life.

In Jesus' name, Amen."

SCRIPTURE REFERENCES

"A slacker will know what it means to be poor, while the hard worker becomes wealthy."

—PROVERBS 10:4 (TPT)

"He becometh poor that dealeth with a slack hand: but the hand of the diligent maketh rich."

—PROVERBS 10:4 (KJV)

"Ruth goes to glean in the fields and works diligently until her favor is noticed."

—RUTH 2:2–7 (KJV/NIV)

"Faith by itself, if it is not accompanied by action, is dead."

—JAMES 2:17 (NIV)

SHE MEANS BUSINESS DECLARATION

- I am diligent, disciplined, and decisive in all I do.
- I step into every opportunity before me with bold confidence.

- My hands are blessed, my labor produces fruit, and my life reflects wealth, prosperity, and abundance.

- I reject procrastination, fear, and worry—I act in faith and power.

DAY 12

SHE'S READY

> Then the Kingdom of Heaven shall be likened unto ten virgins, who took their lamps and went out to meet the bridegroom. Five of them were wise, and five were foolish.
>
> —MATTHEW 25:1 (KJV)

DEVOTIONAL

The Parable of the Ten Virgins is one of Jesus' strongest messages about stewardship, purpose, and preparation. It is faith in action—five of them were wise, and five were foolish. There was a reward for those five virgins who did not waste their time but stayed ready and prepared. Five were foolish because they slept through their season and were not prepared when the bridegroom came.

This story isn't just about the oil—it's about what you do with what God has given you. Your talents, your influence, your voice, your vision—those are your "lamps." God expects you to be diligent with what He has placed in your hands, not bury it in fear, excuses, or procrastination.

Let's be real: too many women of faith are waiting for "the right time" or "more resources" to start. But God says, *"Use what's already in your hand."* You don't need more—just faith as small as a mustard seed will move you forward with what you already have. Notice that the five wise virgins had to go buy more oil to stay prepared for when the time would come. Faith without action is dead. The five foolish women found themselves on the outside looking in.

In Genesis 12, God told Abraham, *"Get up and go."* In other words—get moving. Stop sitting around waiting for something to happen. If it's a door you need opened, go knock on it—or if you know God has something behind it, go kick it down! If you need money, go learn how to earn more. If you need education, figure out how to get it.

We have no excuse today—with all the resources and technology available at our fingertips. Laziness and waiting on someone else to do it for us are causing an abundance of poverty, when prosperity is right at our door. Too many times, we whine about what we lack when we should be learning. The knowledge you need is right in front of you. I often hear people say they don't want to learn new things, yet they go about their day wondering why they aren't making enough money to pay the bills. But here's the truth: what you refuse to steward will eventually be taken and given to someone who will.

Stop waiting for a miracle—**go be the miracle.**

Stop waiting for things to change—**go make change happen.**

Look at the women in Scripture:

- Lydia, in the book of Acts, got saved and immediately opened her home as a church so Paul could preach there.

- Ruth went out and gleaned faithfully every day, positioning herself for favor and blessing.

- The woman at the well became the first woman evangelist—she ran out to tell everyone what Jesus had done.

What are you waiting for? If you think you're waiting on God, don't—He's already far ahead of you. He's waiting on you to step up and take hold of your assignment. God is always on the move—healing someone, saving someone, finding a lost sheep, prospering someone who's faithful.

When I pastored, I thought I was reaching a lot of people. But in the marketplace—on the community mission field—I've touched and ministered to more people than ever came inside the four walls of my church. There's a great, untapped mission field in entrepreneurship. Don't get me wrong, I consider myself as much a minister in the marketplace as I did when I was pastoring. I still preach in churches, Bible schools, and coffee shops. One day, I asked the Lord about my mission and why I wasn't ministering every week like when I was pastoring. He said, *"You are—it just looks different. I've expanded your ministry into the marketplace so you have a broader reach."*

The definition of an apostle is "one sent on a mission"—called into the highways and byways as an advocate, champion, and promoter of His Kingdom. That sounds just like an entrepreneur leading a business—someone sent or given a vision to build something that has never been built, promoted, or proclaimed before. One who compels people. I may be doing business in the marketplace, but I'm doing Kingdom business for God.

Faith is not passive—it's active. God blesses motion, not idleness. You can't steer a parked car, and He can't bless what you refuse to build. God won't do for you what He's already instructed you to do.

So, faithful and ambitious woman—this is your call: find out what you're good at, what you love to do, and go do it. Work what God planted in you. The world needs the gift only you can bring. The Kingdom expands when you step into your assignment and have the courage to get up, show up, and rise up. If you can dream it, you can build it! You already have within you the ability to fulfill your God-given assignment.

So, girlfriend, **grow up, get up, and show up** every day to make the world a better place.

"Faith isn't passive—it's active. God blesses motion, not idleness, He can't bless what you refuse to build."

— Dr. Margo Bush

Faith Action

Today, identify one area in your business, ministry, or personal life where you've been waiting on a "miracle" or "perfect timing."

Take one practical step forward—make the call, send the proposal, start the project, or speak to the right person. Show God your readiness and obedience.

Reflection Questions

1. What talents, resources, or influence has God already placed in your hands that you've been neglecting?

2. Where in your life or business have you been "waiting" instead of stepping into action?

3. How can you prepare now so you are ready when God's opportunity arrives?

4. Who can you serve, teach, or invest in today to expand your Kingdom impact?

Prayer Prompt

"Father, help me to rise ready today. Show me the areas in my life where I have been passive or waiting. Give me the courage to take action, steward what You've entrusted to me, and step into the assignment You've placed before me. Align my heart with Your timing, and let my diligence open doors of favor, blessing, and Kingdom impact.

Day 12 | She's Ready

In Jesus' name, Amen."

Scripture References

Parable of the Ten Virgins:

> *1 Then shall the kingdom of heaven be likened unto ten virgins, which took their lamps, and went forth to meet the bridegroom.*
>
> *2 And five of them were wise, and five were foolish.*
>
> *3 They that were foolish took their lamps, and took no oil with them:*
>
> *4 But the wise took oil in their vessels with their lamps.*
>
> *5 While the bridegroom tarried, they all slumbered and slept.*
>
> *6 And at midnight there was a cry made, Behold, the bridegroom cometh; go ye out to meet him.*
>
> *7 Then all those virgins arose, and trimmed their lamps.*
>
> *8 And the foolish said unto the wise, Give us of your oil; for our lamps are gone out.*
>
> *9 But the wise answered, saying, Not so; lest there be not enough for us and you: but go ye rather to them that sell, and buy for yourselves.*
>
> *10 And while they went to buy, the bridegroom came; and they that were ready went in with him to the marriage: and the door was shut.*
>
> *11 Afterward came also the other virgins, saying, Lord, Lord, open to us.*
>
> *12 But he answered and said, Verily I say unto you, I know you not.*

> *13 Watch therefore, for ye know neither the day nor the hour wherein the Son of man cometh.*
>
> —Matthew 25:1–13 (KJV)

Faith by itself, if it is not accompanied by action, is dead.

—James 2:17 (NIV)

Lydia opened her home and started a church immediately after salvation.

> *And a certain woman named Lydia, a seller of purple, of the city of Thyatira, which worshipped God, heard us: whose heart the Lord opened, that she attended unto the things which were spoken of Paul.*
>
> —Acts 16:14 (KJV)

Ruth went out daily to glean faithfully.

> *And Ruth the Moabitess said unto Naomi, Let me now go to the field, and glean ears of corn after him in whose sight I shall find grace. And she said unto her, Go, my daughter.*
>
> —Ruth 2:2 (KJV)

The woman at the well became an evangelist by taking action.

> *28 The woman then left her waterpot, and went her way into the city, and saith to the men,*
>
> *29 Come, see a man, which told me all things that ever I did: is not this the Christ?*
>
> *30 Then they went out of the city, and came unto him.*
>
> —John 4:28–30 (KJV)

SHE MEANS BUSINESS DECLARATION

- I rise up each morning ready to meet the world and do business with God.

- I steward well what God has placed in my hands with diligence, faith, and action.

- I will not wait for perfection, delay, or fear—I will step into my assignment each day with excitement and faith.

- My lamp is burning, my oil is ready, and I am positioned to receive every opportunity God has for me.

- I get up, rise up, and show up each day ready to fulfill my calling and purpose on this earth.

She Faces Heaven

> But Daniel, brimming with spirit and intelligence, so completely outclassed the other vice-regents and governors that the king decided to put him in charge of the whole kingdom.
>
> —Daniel 6:3 (MSG)

Devotional

When your mornings are given to prayer, success for Kingdom entrepreneurs doesn't come from hustle—it comes from hearing.

Daniel was not just a man of prayer—he was a man of power, purpose, and professionalism. His faith was not limited to the temple; it was evident in the marketplace. He carried himself with such spirit and intelligence that even in a foreign land, he was promoted to the highest levels of leadership.

Scripture says Daniel was brimming with spirit and intelligence. This wasn't mere talent—it was evidence of the divine working through him. His success flowed from diligence, discipline, and devotion. Daniel demanded the best of himself, and his diligence created an atmosphere of excellence in every assignment. God's Spirit operated through his obedience, and his prayer life gave him divine wisdom to govern.

Daniel's morning–noon–night prayer rhythm didn't just shape his worship; it shaped his world. His devotion before God affected divine order in the boardroom, the budget, and every business decision he made.

You too can brim with that same spirit and intelligence. It comes from those sacred early morning hours before the Father. Out of private prayer come purpose, promise, and heartfelt pursuit—qualities that cause others to take notice. When you operate with excellence—showing up prepared, walking in integrity, and making Spirit-led decisions in your business—promotion flows from favor, and destiny becomes clear. His direction is divine direction, not just decision-making.

So, when are the ideal times to prostrate before the Lord and hear heaven's whispers?

The early mornings are the best time. Your mind is open, your heart is most sensitive, and heaven is speaking when the world is sleeping—you will hear heaven's whispers. Morning meditation becomes the moments when the Master is calling you for a meeting, and it's in those intersections that your pathways of purpose are divinely planned.

Psalm 143:8 declares,

> *"Cause me to hear thy lovingkindness in the morning; for in thee do I trust. Cause me to know the way wherein I should walk; for I lift up my soul unto thee."*

The Passion Translation reads,

> *"Let the dawning day bring me revelation of your tender, unfailing love. Give me light for my path and teach me, for I trust in you."*

Let me ask you a question: What if you started treating your mornings like a meeting with the King?

Day 13 | She Faces Heaven

Think of Esther. Before she entered the palace, she prepared herself for days in advance. What if you began the night before—setting up your tomorrow like it was an important boardroom meeting with Heaven?

David did.

Psalm 5:3 (TPT) says, *"At each and every sunrise you will hear my voice as I prepare my sacrifice of prayer to you. Every morning I lay out the pieces of my life on the altar and wait for your fire to fall upon my heart."*

Imagine walking into each day equipped with Heaven's blueprint. You wouldn't just survive your day—you'd command it. You would enter each day with peace and purpose. You wouldn't be asking, *"Lord, where are You?"* or *"Why haven't You shown up?"*—because you would already have met Him before the world woke up.

Here's the wonder: the same Commander-in-Chief who spoke to Deborah to command armies is the same God who called Esther for a purpose in the palace, the same God who met Lydia for a mission, and the same God who is waiting for you in the morning.

What if you looked at each morning not as routine, but as a time of revelation? That's exactly why the enemy tries to steal them with distractions and delays. He knows if he can take your mornings, he can control your momentum. But when you rise with God, no weapon formed against you shall prosper.

Don't treat your mornings in prayer as ordinary, but as an opportunity where Heaven's wisdom becomes your advantage. There is a divine mystery that unfolds when a believer learns to seek God early.

Mark 1:35 says, *"And in the morning, rising up a great while before day, he went out, and departed into a solitary place, and there prayed."*

Jesus modeled this. Every morning, He departed to a solitary place. He knew that miracles didn't come from movement, but from how He spent His mornings. Every healing, every direction, every leading flowed from those early hours.

Before Jesus faced the crowds, He faced the Father.

Before He spoke to man, He spoke to the Master.

Before He handled problems, He sat in God's presence.

Before He gave direction to His disciples, He received direction for His destiny.

Before He dealt with Jewish leaders, He became a world leader in the secret place.

He took those early morning hours to be face-to-face with the Father— so He could go face-to-face with the world.

Like Daniel, your spiritual life and professional life should flow together seamlessly. Pursue His presence so that your life reflects both spirit and intelligence for your purpose. The world may be watching your work, but Heaven is backing your movements.

Your early morning prayer life is where your purpose gets polished and your destiny becomes defined.

"Your faith life and business life should be one seamless flow of pursuing His purpose."

—Dr. Margo Bush

Faith Action

- Prepare your morning meetings, the night before to meet with your Maker.

- Write down three ways you can elevate your intelligence to increase your business this week—through education, coaching, organization, or leadership.

- Commit to operating with the same spirit of excellence that distinguished Daniel.

REFLECTION QUESTIONS

1. What would change in your business, your leadership, and your life if you began to treat every morning like a meeting with the King?

2. How am I currently stewarding my mornings? Am I treating them as sacred time or letting distractions steal them?

3. What talents, opportunities, or visions has God placed in my hands that I'm not fully using?

4. How can I align my professional actions with my spiritual devotion to maximize Kingdom impact?

PRAYER PROMPT

"Father, direct my early times with you so I am ready each day to meet with You first. Give me clarity, wisdom, and courage to act on the instructions You reveal. Help me to better steward my time, my talents, and my opportunities. May my mornings prepare me for divine success and my days reflect Your favor upon my life.

In Jesus' name, Amen."

SCRIPTURE REFERENCES

> *"Then the Kingdom of Heaven shall be likened unto ten virgins, who took their lamps and went out to meet the bridegroom. Five of them were wise, and five were foolish."*
>
> —MATTHEW 25:1–2 (NKJV)

> *"Cause me to hear thy lovingkindness in the morning; for in thee do I trust. Cause me to know the way wherein I should walk; for I lift up my soul unto thee."*
>
> —PSALM 143:8

> *"At each and every sunrise you will hear my voice as I prepare my sacrifice of prayer to you. Every morning I lay*

out the pieces of my life on the altar and wait for your fire to fall upon my heart."

—Psalm 5:3 (TPT)

"And in the morning, rising up a great while before day, he went out, and departed into a solitary place, and there prayed."

—Mark 1:35

SHE MEANS BUSINESS DECLARATION

- I rise up ready and prepared to do business with God.
- I steward my mornings as sacred appointments with God.
- I am diligent, carry a spirit of excellence, make Spirit-led decisions, and step boldly into my assignment with faith each day.
- My mornings set the tone for divine favor, promotion, and supernatural increase.
- I am a Kingdom-minded businesswoman who faces Heaven first—before I face the world.

"When your mornings are given to prayer, success doesn't just come from hustle—it comes from hearing."

—Dr. Margo Bush

ALABASTER BOX

And, behold, a woman in the city, which was a sinner, when she knew that Jesus sat at meat in the Pharisee's house, brought an alabaster box of ointment, And stood at his feet behind him weeping, and began to wash his feet with tears, and did wipe them with the hairs of her head, and kissed his feet, and anointed them with the ointment.

—Luke 7:37–38 (KJV)

DEVOTIONAL

This woman had a reputation. Everyone in the city knew who she was —a sinner, a prostitute, a woman whose name was whispered in judgment. But one day, she heard that Jesus was nearby, dining in the house of a respected religious leader. Something deep inside her refused to stay hidden any longer. She ran to Him—desperate for forgiveness, peace, and a new life.

Her heart was so broken over her past that she didn't care what others thought. She pushed past shame, rejection, and fear of opinion. She entered the home uninvited, fell at His feet, and began to worship—

weeping, washing His feet with her tears, and pouring out her most expensive perfume. She gave Jesus everything she had because she understood who He was: her Savior, her Peace, her Redeemer—the Great I Am.

Many women in business today have their own version of this story. Some were delivered from addiction. Others came out of incarceration, abuse, or years of lack and struggle. Some started a business because no one would hire them. But now, they stand as successful entrepreneurs —women clothed in grace, walking in freedom and favor, because of Jesus.

Like the woman with the alabaster box, you know what it feels like to be forgiven much. You know what it feels like to be restored when others counted you out. That's why your success is not just a business accomplishment—it's a testimony. It's worship.

Every sale, every client, every opportunity is a chance to pour out your gratitude before the Lord. Never lose that sense of reverence. Don't let your success make you forget your Savior. Whether your sins were great or small, the price He paid was the same—and your worship should always reflect the depth of your gratitude.

The religious leaders in that room were too proud to recognize who sat before them. But this woman saw clearly what they could not: Jesus is the Great I Am—the only One who can take a broken life and make it beautiful.

I love the song *"Alabaster Box"* by CeCe Winans, inspired by the story of this woman. Written by Janice Sjostrand, the lyrics paint a picture of deep, personal worship—the kind that flows from a heart that remembers where God found her. One line stands out to me:

> *"You don't know the cost of the oil in my alabaster box."*

This line reminds us that true worship always costs something. It's the surrender of pride, the breaking of self, the pouring out of everything we are in gratitude for all He's done.

A dear friend of mine was delivered out of sex trafficking, and her husband was set free from a life of drugs, addiction, and sin. Their gratitude is so evident every time I see them. They were both so far from

God, yet when He found them and set them free, they gave all of themselves to Jesus.

To them, these words mean everything: *"You don't know the cost—you have no idea the cost. If you only knew the price that Jesus' blood paid for me, and how grateful I am that He came looking for me and found me in my wretched state."*

What does this have to do with business? Everything. If you only knew the price He paid for your success, prosperity, and abundance, you would never entertain a lack-minded thought again.

"When Jesus delivers you from much, worship becomes your language and gratitude becomes your lifestyle."

—Dr. Margo Bush

Faith Action

- Spend a few moments today in worship, not asking God for anything— just thanking Him for everything.

- Write down three ways Jesus has changed your life and business.

- Give Him praise for where He's brought you from and where He's taking you.

- Consider blessing someone who's still on their journey out of bondage —your generosity becomes part of their healing.

Reflection Questions

1. What has God delivered you from that fuels your gratitude today?

2. In what ways can you turn your daily work into worship?

3. Have you allowed success to distract you from the Source of your blessing?

Prayer Prompt

"Lord, thank You for redeeming my life from destruction and giving me beauty for ashes. Help me to never forget the cost of my freedom. May my business, my work, and my success be a continual act of worship before You. Keep my heart pure and grateful, always remembering that everything I have comes from You.

In Jesus' name, Amen."

Scripture References

37 And, behold, a woman in the city, which was a sinner, when she knew that Jesus sat at meat in the Pharisee's house, brought an alabaster box of ointment,

38 And stood at his feet behind him weeping, and began to wash his feet with tears, and did wipe them with the hairs of her head, and kissed his feet, and anointed them with the ointment.

—Luke 7:37–38 (KJV)

2 Praise the Lord, my soul,
 and forget not all his benefits—

3 who forgives all your sins
 and heals all your diseases,

4 who redeems your life from the pit
 and crowns you with love and compassion,

5 who satisfies your desires with good things
 so that your youth is renewed like the eagle's.

—Psalm 103:2–5 (NIV)

23 Whatever you do, work at it with all your heart, as working for the Lord, not for human masters, 24 since you know that you will receive an inheritance from the Lord as a reward. It is the Lord Christ you are serving.

—Colossians 3:23–24 (NIV)

Glorify God with all your wealth, honoring him with your firstfruits, with every increase that comes to you. [10] Then every dimension of your life will overflow with blessings from an uncontainable source of inner joy!

—Proverbs 3:9–10 (TPT)

She Means Business Declaration

I will work as unto the Lord, today and every day.

My business is my alabaster box—a gift poured out for His glory and my gratitude.

Daily Confession

- I remember what the Lord has done for me, and I give Him all the glory.

- My business is a testimony of His covenant promise to me—He leads me into success.

- I am free, forgiven, and favored by God.

- I give my best daily and work as unto the Lord—my time, my talents, my treasure.

SHE HAS A KINGDOM-MINDSET

> But seek first the Kingdom of God and His righteousness, and all these things will be added to you.
>
> —MATTHEW 6:33 (KJV)

DEVOTIONAL

True prosperity begins with focus. Matthew 6:33 calls us to *seek first the Kingdom of God and His righteousness*. This is not just a spiritual suggestion—it is a divine life and business principle that governs success in the way we should walk out our lives on this earth. When the Kingdom is first, every decision, strategy, and relationship becomes aligned with God's Kingdom.

Seeking the Kingdom first means making God your ultimate life and business partner. It means consulting Him in the early morning, making prayer a part of your *life*, not just a time you set aside. It's allowing your daily communication with Him to guide your decisions, contracts, and investments. It's seeking His wisdom over every opportunity and prioritizing integrity over immediate gain.

A Kingdom mindset shifts the focus from what is *urgent* to what is *eternal*—from chasing outcomes to following divine direction. When the Kingdom is first, "all these things"—resources, opportunities, favor, and influence—are added. Wealth, promotion, and business growth are not accidental; they flow naturally when your actions and words are rooted in God's righteousness.

It is the alignment of faith, work, and strategy that creates sustainable success.

A woman with a Kingdom mindset approaches her work with intentionality, stewardship, and vision. She recognizes that her business is not just a source of income—it is a platform for Kingdom outcome that will outshine her income. Her life is focused, ready to serve her community, and impact nations. Her decisions are informed by skill and intelligence, her words carry authority, and her actions reflect both God's principles and Kingdom purpose.

Kingdom-minded decisions often look counterintuitive in the natural—they may require patience, generosity, or risk. But God's promise is clear: when His Kingdom comes first, He will provide the resources, connections, and favor needed to fulfill your God-given life and business dreams.

A Woman with a Kingdom Mindset—The Shunammite Woman (2 Kings 4:8–37)

The Shunammite woman beautifully models what it means to live with a Kingdom mindset. She was a woman of means, but more importantly, she was a woman of discernment. When the prophet Elisha often passed through her town, she recognized that he was a man of God and chose to create space for the presence of God in her home. She didn't wait for instruction—she acted from revelation.

She said to her husband, *"Let's make a small room on the roof and furnish it for him with a bed, a table, a chair, and a lamp."* (2 Kings 4:10) Her generosity wasn't driven by what she could gain, but by her desire to honor God's Kingdom and presence.

Her hospitality became the doorway to her miracle. Though she had no son and her husband was old, the prophet declared, *"About this time next year, you will hold a son in your arms."*

Day 15 | She Has a Kingdom-Mindset

When her son later died suddenly, this woman didn't panic. She didn't speak words of defeat. Instead, she declared, *"It is well."* That is the language of a Kingdom mindset. She believed that if God gave her the promise, He was also faithful to sustain it.

She sought the man of God again—not from desperation, but with determination. And God honored her faith. Her son was raised from the dead.

The Shunammite woman teaches us that when we make room for God's Kingdom first—when we sow into what honors His presence—He multiplies back life, blessing, and abundance beyond what we can imagine.

Kingdom women don't chase opportunities; they create space for God, and opportunity comes chasing them.

"A Kingdom-mindset doesn't chase success—it creates it."

—Dr. Margo Bush

Faith Action

Spend intentional time this week inviting God into every area of your business. Write down the areas where you've been striving and instead surrender them to divine alignment. Ask the Holy Spirit for one specific instruction to *seek first* His way—and obey it immediately.

1. Take a concrete action step this week to align that area with God's will—pray over it, restructure it, or bless it.

2. Identify one area in your business where Kingdom principles can be applied more intentionally—ethics, client relationships, hiring, or giving.

3. Journal how you see God responding as you prioritize His Kingdom above immediate results.

Reflection Questions

1. What does "seeking first the Kingdom" look like in your business decisions?

2. Where have you been anxious about provision instead of trusting His promise to add "all these things"?

3. How can you create more "space" for God's presence in your daily business flow, as the Shunammite woman did?

Prayer Prompt

"Father, thank You for teaching me to live with a Kingdom mindset. I will keep you first in all things—my time, my goals, my finances, and my decisions. I seek Your will above my own; everything I need will be added to me. Align my business with the assignment on my life so that my work becomes a witness of Your abundance and prosperity.

In Jesus' name, Amen."

Scripture References

If God gives such attention to the appearance of wildflowers—most of which are never even seen—don't you think he'll attend to you, take pride in you, do his best for you? What I'm trying to do here is to get you to relax, to not be so preoccupied with getting, so you can respond to God's giving. People who don't know God and the way he works fuss over these things, but you know both God and how he works. Steep your life in God-reality, God-initiative, God-provisions. Don't worry about missing out. You'll find all your everyday human concerns will be met.

—Matthew 6:30–33 (MSG)

8 Now there came a day when Elisha went over to Shunem, where there was a prominent and influential woman, and she persuaded him to eat a meal. Afterward, whenever he passed by, he stopped there for a meal. 9 She said to her husband, "Behold, I sense that this is a holy man of God who frequently passes our way. 10 Please, let us make a

DAY 15 | SHE HAS A KINGDOM-MINDSET

small, fully-walled upper room [on the housetop] and put a bed there for him, with a table, a chair, and a lampstand. Then whenever he comes to visit us, he can turn in there."

11 One day he came there and turned in to the upper room and lay down to rest. 12 And he said to Gehazi his servant, "Call this Shunammite." So he called her and she stood before him. 13 Now he said to Gehazi, "Say to her now, 'You have gone to all this trouble for us; what can I do for you? Would you like to be mentioned to the king or to the captain of the army?'" She answered, "I live among my own people [in peace and security and need no special favors]." 14 Later Elisha said, "What then is to be done for her?" Gehazi answered, "Well, she has no son and her husband is old." 15 He said, "Call her." So Gehazi called her, and she [came and] stood in the doorway. 16 Elisha said, "At this season next year, you will embrace a son." She said, "No, my lord. O man of God, do not lie to your maidservant."

17 But the woman conceived and gave birth to a son at that season the next year, just as Elisha had said to her.

18 When the child was grown, the day came that he went out to his father, to the reapers. 19 But he said to his father, "My head, my head." The man said to his servant, "Carry him to his mother." 20 When he had carried and brought him to his mother, he sat on her lap until noon, and then he died. 21 She went up and laid him on the bed of the man of God, and shut the door [of the small upper room] behind him and left. 22 Then she called to her husband and said, "Please send me one of the servants and one of the donkeys, so that I may run to the man of God and return." 23 He said, "Why are you going to him today? It is neither the New Moon nor the Sabbath." And she said, "It will be all right." 24 Then she saddled the donkey and said to her servant, "Drive [the animal] fast; do not slow down the pace for me unless I tell you." 25 So she set out and came to the man of God at Mount Carmel.

When the man of God saw her at a distance, he said to Gehazi his servant, "Look, there is the Shunammite woman. 26 Please run now to meet her and ask her, 'Is it well with you? Is it well with your husband? Is it well with the child?'" And she answered, "It is well." 27 When she came to the mountain to the man of God, she took hold of his feet. Gehazi approached to push her away; but the man of God said, "Let her alone, for her soul is desperate and troubled within her; and the Lord has hidden the reason from me and has not told me." 28 Then she said, "Did I ask for a son from my lord? Did I not say, 'Do not give me false hope'?"

29 Then he said to Gehazi, "Gird up your loins (prepare now!) and take my staff in your hand, and go [to the woman's house]; if you meet any man [along the way], do not greet him and if a man greets you, do not [stop to] answer him; and lay my staff on the face of the boy [as soon as you reach the house]." 30 The mother of the child said, "As the Lord lives and as your soul lives, I will not leave you." So Elisha arose and followed her. 31 Gehazi went on ahead of them and laid the staff on the boy's face, but there was no sound or response [from the boy]. So he turned back to meet Elisha and told him, "The boy has not awakened (revived)."

32 When Elisha came into the house, the child was dead and lying on his bed. 33 So he went in, shut the door behind the two of them, and prayed to the Lord. 34 Then he went up and lay on the child and put his mouth on his mouth, his eyes on his eyes, and his hands on his hands. And as he stretched himself out on him and held him, the boy's skin became warm. 35 Then he returned and walked in the house once back and forth, and went up [again] and stretched himself out on him; and the boy sneezed seven times and he opened his eyes. 36 Then Elisha called Gehazi and said, "Call this Shunammite." So he called her. And when she came to him, he said, "Pick up your son." 37 She came and fell at his feet, bowing herself to the ground [in respect and gratitude]. Then she picked up her son and left.

—2 Kings 4:8–37 (AMP)

Trust in the Lord completely, and do not rely on your own opinions. With all your heart rely on him to guide you, and he will lead you in every decision you make. [6] Become intimate with him in whatever you do, and he will lead you wherever you go.

—Proverbs 3:5–6 (TPT)

And my God will meet all your needs according to the riches of his glory in Christ Jesus.

—Philippians 4:19 (NIV)

She Means Business Declaration

- I am a Kingdom-minded entrepreneur—I follow God's Way of doing business.

- I was born for greatness—I was born for purpose.

- My business is built on divine alignment with my destiny—not stress and striving.

- I have favor, provision, and influence because I operate from a place of faith, wisdom, and purpose.

"When God is your CEO, favor becomes your currency and purpose becomes your profit."

—Dr. Margo Bush

SHE STEPS INTO ABUNDANCE

> Beloved, I pray that in every way you may succeed and prosper and be in good health [physically], just as [I know] your soul prospers [spiritually].
>
> —3 John 1:2 (AMP)

DEVOTIONAL

God's desire for your life is not partial prosperity—it's complete prosperity. Spirit, soul, and body. In 3 John 1:2, the Apostle John reveals the divine will of God for every believer: that we would *prosper in all things and be in good health*, even as our soul prospers.

Too many believers stop short, believing this verse speaks only of spiritual growth. But it's much bigger than that. God is saying, "As your inner life flourishes, everything connected to you will flourish too."

Your **soul**—your mind, will, and emotions—is the control center of your life. When your soul prospers, your decisions become sharper, your emotions steadier, and your faith stronger. A prosperous soul

attracts divine ideas, strategies, and resources that align with God's Kingdom. Prosperity doesn't begin in your bank account—it begins in your belief system.

When your inner life is thriving, your business life will thrive. A calm, faith-filled soul can hear God clearly. It's not tossed by fear, worry, or lack. Instead, it's anchored in divine confidence. From that place, creativity flows. Wisdom flows. Strategy flows. And abundance follows.

A prosperous soul doesn't strive—it strategizes with the Spirit. You stop asking, *"How will this happen?"* and start declaring, *"God is faithful to complete what He started in me."*

Psalm 5:8 reminds us, *"Lead me, O Lord, in Your righteousness because of my enemies; make Your way straight before me."* God smooths the road ahead when we seek His direction. He removes obstacles, clarifies steps, and aligns our pace with His will.

When your soul prospers, your next step isn't just forward—it's forward in *favor, fulfillment, and freedom.*

The Proverbs 31 Woman

The Proverbs 31 woman is a living example of soul prosperity manifesting in every area of life. She was not driven by hustle but by harmony—her faith, wisdom, and diligence worked together to produce abundance.

Scripture says she *"rises while it is yet night"* (v.15), meaning she starts her day in alignment with purpose. She *"considers a field and buys it; out of her earnings she plants a vineyard"* (v.16). That's strategic entrepreneurship, not happenstance.

Her prosperity flowed from her inner life—strength, vision, and faith. She didn't operate out of fear of the future but out of confidence in her God. *"She is clothed with strength and dignity, and she laughs without fear of the future."* (v.25 NLT)

This woman was wealthy in wisdom, rich in purpose, and generous in spirit. Her abundance was not only financial—it was emotional, spiritual, and generational. Her family, employees, and community all benefited from the overflow of her prosperous soul.

That's the Kingdom way. When your soul prospers, your business prospers. When your business prospers, others are blessed. And when others are blessed, God is glorified.

You are that woman. You are the modern Proverbs 31 entrepreneur—filled with faith, guided by vision, and empowered by wisdom. When your soul is aligned with Heaven, abundance isn't forced—it flows.

"When your soul prospers—success has no choice but to follow."

—Dr. Margo Bush

FAITH ACTION

Take a few moments today to journal what prosperity means to you beyond money. Where do you need your soul to prosper—your thoughts, emotions, confidence, or creativity? Then, ask God to renew that area. Declare that your inner growth will manifest in outward fruitfulness.

1. Spend 10 minutes today journaling what "soul prosperity" looks like for you. Identify one area of your life that needs attention—spirit, soul, or body—and take one step to nurture it.

2. Ask God to reveal your next business step and write it down. Pray for clarity, favor, and strategy as you move forward.

REFLECTION QUESTIONS

1. What does a "prosperous soul" look like in your daily life and business?

2. Where have you allowed fear, stress, or lack-mindset to limit your abundance?

3. How can you create space daily for your mind, will, and emotions to align with God's truth?

Prayer Prompt

"Father, thank You that Your desire for me is to prosper and be in health as my soul prospers. Teach me to walk in abundance from the inside out. Heal my thoughts, strengthen my will, and renew my emotions so I can align with Your wisdom and direction. I receive divine ideas, Kingdom strategies, and supernatural favor. I step boldly into the abundance You've already prepared for me.

In Jesus' name, Amen."

Scripture References

Beloved, I wish above all things that thou mayest prosper and be in health, even as thy soul prospereth.

—3 John 1:2 (KJV)

Beloved, I pray that in every way you may succeed and prosper and be in good health [physically], just as [I know] your soul prospers [spiritually].

—3 John 1:2 (AMP)

10 An excellent woman [one who is spiritual, capable, intelligent, and virtuous], who is he who can find her? Her value is more precious than jewels and her worth is far above rubies or pearls.

11 The heart of her husband trusts in her [with secure confidence], And he will have no lack of gain.

12 She comforts, encourages, and does him only good and not evil All the days of her life.

13 She looks for wool and flax And works with willing hands in delight.

DAY 16 | SHE STEPS INTO ABUNDANCE

14 She is like the merchant ships [abounding with treasure]; She brings her [household's] food from far away.

*15 She rises also while it is still night
And gives food to her household
And assigns tasks to her maids.*

*16 She considers a field before she buys or accepts it [expanding her business prudently];
With her profits she plants fruitful vines in her vineyard.*

17 She equips herself with strength [spiritual, mental, and physical fitness for her God-given task] And makes her arms strong.

*18 She sees that her gain is good;
Her lamp does not go out, but it burns continually through the night [she is prepared for whatever lies ahead].*

*19 She stretches out her hands to the distaff,
And her hands hold the spindle [as she spins wool into thread for clothing].*

*20 She opens and extends her hand to the poor,
And she reaches out her filled hands to the needy.*

*21 She does not fear the snow for her household,
For all in her household are clothed in [expensive] scarlet [wool].*

22 She makes for herself coverlets, cushions, and rugs of tapestry. Her clothing is linen, pure and fine, and purple [wool].

*23 Her husband is known in the [city's] gates,
When he sits among the elders of the land.*

*24 She makes [fine] linen garments and sells them;
And supplies sashes to the merchants.*

25 Strength and dignity are her clothing and her position is strong and secure; And she smiles at the future [knowing that she and her family are prepared].

*26 She opens her mouth in [skillful and godly] wisdom,
And the teaching of kindness is on her tongue [giving counsel and instruction].*

*27 She looks well to how things go in her household,
And does not eat the bread of idleness.*

28 Her children rise up and call her blessed (happy, prosperous, to be admired); Her husband also, and he praises her, saying,

*29 "Many daughters have done nobly, and well [with the strength of character that is steadfast in goodness],
But you excel them all."*

30 Charm and grace are deceptive, and [superficial] beauty is vain, But a woman who fears the Lord [reverently worshiping, obeying, serving, and trusting Him with awe-filled respect], she shall be praised.

*31 Give her of the product of her hands,
And let her own works praise her in the gates [of the city].*

—P<small>ROVERBS</small> 31:10–31 (AMP)

YAHWEH, lead me in the pathways of your pleasure just like you promised me you would, or else my enemies will conquer me. Smooth out your road in front of me, straight and level, so that I will know where to walk.

—P<small>SALM</small> 5:8 (TPT)

And my God will meet all your needs according to the riches of his glory in Christ Jesus.

—P<small>HILIPPIANS</small> 4:19 (NIV)

S<small>HE</small> M<small>EANS</small> B<small>USINESS</small> D<small>ECLARATION</small>

- My soul prospers, therefore my life and business prosper.

Day 16 | She Steps Into Abundance

- I am full of confidence and live in alignment with the divine destiny that is on my life

- Business strategies, inventions, and ideas flow to me to build a successful business.

- I am not striving for success—I am stepping into abundance.

DAY 17

HER MILLION DOLLAR CHALLENGE

And Elisha said unto her, What shall I do for thee? Tell me, what hast thou in the house? And she said, Thine handmaid hath not any thing in the house, save a pot of oil..

—2 KINGS 4:2 (KJV)

DEVOTIONAL

Every year, I challenge my students to take what I call **The Million Dollar Challenge**—a challenge rooted in the principles found in 2 Kings 4:3–7. In this story, the prophet Elisha charged the widow woman to take bold, obedient action in faith—and it unlocked her blessing.

I'll never forget when my own coach challenged me to make **$10,000 in 10 days**. At first, I thought it was impossible. But I quickly learned something powerful: when you decide to believe in what God has placed within you, your capacity expands. You begin to see possibilities where there once were only limitations.

The truth is—most people are living far below their God-given potential. If you only knew what was already inside of you, you would stop struggling and start thriving.

When I first started my business journey in 2010, I had no idea I could do what I'm doing today. But I made a decision to stop making excuses. I worked harder than ever to learn, to grow, and to connect with people who could teach me. I stopped thinking small.

I once heard a great businessman say, "Stop thinking small. It's just as hard—if not harder—to think small as it is to think big. Go after big deals, big projects, and big money."

That's the power of mindset—**90% of making money is mental**.

The widow woman had to step out of her comfort zone. She had to move past fear—fear of failure, fear of what others might say, and fear of her own self-doubt—and she had to **obey every instruction** from the prophet.

Step 1: Elisha gave her instruction that was simple, yet challenging:

> "Go up and down the street and borrow jugs and bowls from all your neighbors. And not just a few—all you can get."

That command stretched her faith. It forced her to take action, to ask, to move, and to trust that God would meet her.

Just like the widow woman, your blessing will begin to flow when you move in obedience and expectation. Realize that this woman had not seen yet what was about to happen. She went merely on obedience and trust. She could have said, "But…" or "What if…" She didn't do any of those things, which I am sure she was tempted to—but instead she started knocking on doors. You'll find out how much you trust God and His word, when He begins asking you to take action. Why? Because He knows how much you are capable of and what is already inside of you—more than you ever imagined.

Step 2: Lock the Door and Pour

"Then come home and lock the door behind you, you and your sons. Pour oil into each container; when each is full, set it aside." 2 Kings 4:4 (MSG)

After gathering every jar she could find, Elisha gave the widow a strange instruction—*lock the door and begin to pour.*

Why? Because not every miracle happens in public. Some blessings are born behind closed doors. Where it's just you and God. He will do more for you than you ever imagine when you get alone with Him and obey.

This was the moment where her *faith met her action*. She had done the uncomfortable part—asking neighbors for jars—but now she had to trust God in private. The prophet told her to shut the door because faith requires focus. When God is about to multiply what's in your hand, He doesn't need an audience—He needs your obedience.

The widow woman and her sons worked together. She poured, and they brought the vessels. It was a family effort, an act of unity and agreement. Sometimes your miracle requires partnership. You can't do it all alone—but you also can't let just anyone in the room.

When I think back to seasons where God was multiplying my work—businesses, students, or opportunities—He often had me *"lock the door."* Not physically, but spiritually. I had to quiet the noise, ignore the opinions, and focus on my obedience to Him.

There's a time for visibility and a time for *privacy*. A time to market your business and a time to go silent and build behind the scenes. The widow's pouring season wasn't about showing off; it was about stewarding. She poured until every single jar was filled—and only then did the oil stop.

Here's the truth:

As long as she had room, the oil kept flowing.

As long as you keep showing up—creating, serving, giving, building—God will keep multiplying what's in your hands. But once you stop making room, once you stop pouring, the flow will begin to stop. It's not too late to start that business. It's not over just because things didn't work out the first time. Make room again for your abundance is drawing

MEANS BUSINESS

near. Start pouring out what God has gifted you with you to change the world.

Step 3: Sell the Oil and Live on What's Left

> *"When all the jugs and bowls were full, she said to one of her sons, 'Another jug, please.' He said, 'That's it. There are no more jugs.' Then the oil stopped. She went and told the story to the man of God. He said, 'Go sell the oil and make good on your debts. Live, both you and your sons, on what's left.'"*
>
> —2 Kings 4:7 (MSG)

Once the miracle had happened, the widow did the right thing—*she went back to the man of God for direction.* That's wisdom. Too many people stop after the miracle, but true stewardship begins when you ask God, *"What do I do next, Lord?"*

The Prophet gave her clear instruction:

Go sell. Pay. Live.

That's a three-part strategy for prosperity and purpose.

1. **Go Sell the Oil.**

    The miracle wasn't just meant for survival—it was meant for the marketplace. The oil represented value, and Elisha told her to *monetize the miracle*. That's a word for someone today: what God gave you is valuable. Your skills, your story, your products, your wisdom—that's your oil. Don't let it sit on a shelf. Go sell it. Go share it. Go release it to the world.

2. **Make Good on Your Debts.**

    Before she could live in overflow, she had to bring order. God blesses what's in alignment with His principles—and part of that is financial integrity. Paying off debt wasn't just about money; it was about *freedom*. God doesn't want you bound. He wants you *free* to live, give, and serve fully.

3. **Live on What's Left.**

   This is the part that speaks to me every time—she didn't just have enough to pay her bills. She had enough to *live a full life*. Financial security for the widow woman and her children. Think about it—that was a lot of oil to live the rest of her life on—it was her overflow. That means God didn't just meet her need; He provided for her future. The same God who fills your jars will give you *financial security and sustainability.*

The widow went from *crying out for help* to *running her own oil business*. She became the solution to her own problem because she obeyed the Solution Maker. *God won't do for you, what He's already told you to do.*

That's how the blessing works—it multiplies what you have, eliminates what binds you, and creates a storehouse for your abundance.

"When God is about to multiply what's in your hand, He doesn't need an audience—He needs your obedience."

—Dr. Margo Bush

Faith Action

1. Gather Your Jars—Identify what resources, skills, or relationships you have and are willing to use to step into your blessing.

2. Lock the Door and Pour—Take intentional, focused action in private, without distraction or fear of judgment.

3. Sell and Steward—Use your blessing wisely, repay what you owe, and live in the overflow.

Reflection Questions

1. What "jars" (resources, gifts, talents) has God already given you that are ready to be used?

2. Are you willing to take private, focused action in faith, even when no one is watching?

3. How can you steward the blessings God provides to impact both yourself and others?

Prayer Prompt

"Lord, help me to gather what You've placed in my hands, pour it out in obedience, and steward the overflow wisely. Teach me to act in faith, trust in Your provision, and live in Your abundance.

In Jesus' name, Amen."

Scripture References

1 One day the wife of a man from the guild of prophets called out to Elisha, "Your servant my husband is dead. You well know what a good man he was, devoted to God. And now the man to whom he was in debt is on his way to collect by taking my two children as slaves."

2 Elisha said, "I wonder how I can be of help. Tell me, what do you have in your house?"

"Nothing," she said. "Well, I do have a little oil."

3-4 "Here's what you do," said Elisha. "Go up and down the street and borrow jugs and bowls from all your neighbors. And not just a few—all you can get. Then come home and lock the door behind you, you and your sons. Pour oil into each container; when each is full, set it aside."

5-6 She did what he said. She locked the door behind her and her sons; as they brought the containers to her, she filled them. When all the jugs and bowls were full, she said to one of her sons, "Another jug, please."

He said, "That's it. There are no more jugs."

Then the oil stopped.

7 She went and told the story to the man of God. He said, "Go sell the oil and make good on your debts. Live, both you and your sons, on what's left."

—2 Kings 4:1–7 (MSG)

1 The wife of a man from the company of the prophets cried out to Elisha, "Your servant my husband is dead, and you know that he revered the Lord. But now his creditor is coming to take my two boys as his slaves."

2 Elisha replied to her, "How can I help you? Tell me, what do you have in your house?"

"Your servant has nothing there at all," she said, "except a small jar of olive oil."

3 Elisha said, "Go around and ask all your neighbors for empty jars. Don't ask for just a few. 4 Then go inside and shut the door behind you and your sons. Pour oil into all the jars, and as each is filled, put it to one side."

5 She left him and shut the door behind her and her sons. They brought the jars to her and she kept pouring. 6 When all the jars were full, she said to her son, "Bring me another one."

But he replied, "There is not a jar left." Then the oil stopped flowing.

7 She went and told the man of God, and he said, "Go, sell the oil and pay your debts. You and your sons can live on what is left."

—2 Kings 4:1–7 (NIV)

Now one of the wives of a man of the sons of the prophets cried out to Elisha [for help], saying "Your servant my husband is dead, and you know that your servant [reverently] feared the Lord; but the creditor is coming to take my two sons to be his slaves [in payment for a loan]." 2 Elisha said to her, "What shall I do for you? Tell me, what do you have [of value] in the house?" She said, "Your maidservant has nothing in the house except a [small] jar of [olive] oil." 3 Then he said, "Go, borrow containers from all your neighbors, empty containers—and not just a few. 4 Then you shall go in and shut the door behind you and your sons, and pour out [the oil you have] into all these containers, and you shall set aside each one when it is full." 5 So she left him and shut the door behind her and her sons; they were bringing her the containers as she poured [the oil]. 6 When the containers were all full, she said to her son, "Bring me another container." And he said to her, "There is not a one left." Then the oil stopped [multiplying]. 7 Then she came and told the man of God. He said, "Go, sell the oil and pay your debt, and you and your sons can live on the rest."

—2 Kings 4:1–7 (AMP)

SHE MEANS BUSINESS DECLARATION

- I abound in abundance in my business and my finances.

- I declare today—the Lord is working on my behalf even when I can't see it to bring my life and business into abundance.

- I step out in faith and obey the leading and promoting of God.

- I trust the Lord to lead me in my life and my business.

WOMEN OF VICTORY

> And take the helmet of salvation, and the sword of the Spirit, which is the word of God.
>
> —EPHESIANS 6:17 (KJV)

DEVOTIONAL

Every woman called to build a business will face battles—spiritual, emotional, and financial—but you were never called to fight empty-handed. God has equipped you with the *sword of the Spirit*, His living Word, to speak victory over every challenge that arises.

Faith isn't just believing that God *can*—it's standing firm in the truth that He *will*. When fear, lack, or opposition show up in your business or life, the Word of God becomes your greatest weapon. It cuts through doubt, confusion, and lies. It silences the enemy and strengthens your spirit.

As a woman of faith in business, you must be both **filled with faith** and **armed with the Word**. The sword only has power when it's spoken.

Declare it. Wield it. Speak it with authority. Every promise of God is a decree waiting for your agreement.

Battles are inevitable, but victory is *promised* to those who stand on the Word. The Word steadies your emotions, strengthens your resolve, and guides your next move. When you put on the whole armor of God, you don't just defend—you advance. Every faith-filled word you speak pushes darkness back and ushers in light, order, and breakthrough.

You are not a victim of circumstance—you are a victorious daughter, clothed in strength and armed with truth. The same Word that created the universe is the Word that will bring you through every battle into prosperity and peace.

"Faith is your fuel, the Word is your weapon, and every battle you face is a setup for your next comeback."

—Dr. Margo Bush

Faith Action

- Identify one area in your business or life that feels like a battle. Write down **three scriptures** that speak directly to that situation.

- Declare those scriptures out loud every day this week.

- Pray in faith, thanking God for the victory *before* you see it.

Reflection Questions

1. What is one battle I am currently facing that requires me to use the Word of God more intentionally?

2. Have I been reacting to my challenges emotionally or responding with faith and scripture?

3. What does "putting on the whole armor of God" look like in my daily business life?

4. How can I build a habit of speaking the Word before speaking my worries?

PRAYER PROMPT

"Father, thank You for equipping me with Your Word as my weapon of victory. Fill me with faith that cannot be shaken. Teach me to stand firm in battle, declaring Your promises until I see breakthrough. Clothe me daily in Your armor—truth, righteousness, peace, faith, salvation, and the Word. Strengthen my hands to war and my voice to declare victory. I trust that every battle I face will end in triumph, for You fight for me.

In Jesus' name, Amen."

SCRIPTURE REFERENCES

"Above all, taking the shield of faith, wherewith ye shall be able to quench all the fiery darts of the wicked."

—EPHESIANS 6:16 (KJV)

"And take the helmet of salvation, and the sword of the Spirit, which is the Word of God [spoken word from God]."

—EPHESIANS 6:17 (AMP)

"And take the helmet of salvation, and the sword of the Spirit, which is the word of God."

—EPHESIANS 6:17 (KJV)

SHE MEANS BUSINESS DECLARATION

- I am full of faith and stand firm in what God's Word says about me and my business—abundance.

- The Word of God is active in my mouth and mighty in power to deliver.

- No weapon formed against my business or destiny will prosper.

- I am clothed in the full armor of God—strong, steady, and victorious.

Her Gift Opens Doors

Would you like to meet a very important person? Take a generous gift. It will do wonders to gain entrance into his presence.

—Proverbs 18:16 (TPT)

Devotional

Divine connections are one of the greatest catalysts for growth. God will often use relationships, meetings, and moments of favor to unlock the next level of your destiny. Proverbs 18:16 teaches us that **a generous gift opens doors**—not just physical doors, but doors of opportunity, influence, and favor.

A generous "gift" doesn't have to be a lot; it can also be your **skill, service, honor, or time**—something of value that you bring to the table. God designed your gifts to make room for you—to place you before people who can expand your knowledge, sharpen your business acumen, and elevate your vision.

As a businesswoman, become sensitive to divine timing and divine placement. There are **"very important people"** God has already positioned along your path—mentors, investors, clients, and teachers—who carry something you need to expand. Listen to God leading you into their presence, and to come prepared, both spiritually and professionally.

As the new year of 2022 approached, I sought the Lord about the next steps for my life and business. I pursued a clear direction for how to expand and move forward. During that time, the Lord impressed upon my heart to begin attending a specific ministers meeting every time they gathered in their hometown. I knew it was a divine instruction and assignment.

So I obeyed; month after month, I attended those meetings. In the natural, nothing remarkable seemed to be happening—no major breakthroughs, no dramatic shifts—just powerful teaching and a consistent time in God's presence. But each time I went, I took a generous gift, sowing into the Word and honoring the prompting of the Holy Spirit. What I didn't realize then was that God was preparing the ground beneath my feet for a greater season of expansion.

By the end of the second year, the Lord began to speak clearly to me about my next assignment—and it was big. It was time to take the business to a new level, a level that required bold faith and even bolder confidence. Looking back, I see how every trip, every teaching, and every act of obedience positioned me for that moment. God was building capacity in me long before I saw the new assignment.

It pays to obey, even when you don't understand what the Lord is doing. Every step of obedience plants a seed for your next season. You may not see it right away, but God always sees ahead—and when the time is right, He reveals the purpose behind the preparation.

Generosity unlocks favor. Honor opens hearts. When you bring your best—not just what's convenient—you demonstrate the Kingdom principle of **seedtime and harvest**. Sometimes your best is—you. You just showing up produces favor. When you sow your time, respect, and money, your return multiplies in influence and prosperity.

Don't be afraid to invest in relationships that stretch you. Attend that conference, reach out to that leader, enroll in that course, send that thoughtful gift or thank-you note. Each act of generosity becomes a bridge that God uses to connect you to the people who will help expand your business and sharpen your understanding of wealth and riches.

Seek the Lord's leading. He knows exactly who you need to meet, when you need to meet them, and how to prepare for that moment. Your gift will do wonders—not because of manipulation, but because of divine favor and obedience.

"Generosity is not just good business—it's divine strategy that invites Heaven's favor to open supernatural doors."

—Dr. Margo Bush

Faith Action

Ask God to highlight one "very important person" you need to connect with in this season—someone whose wisdom, experience, or influence can help you grow.

- Prepare a **seed of honor**—a gift, gesture, or message that communicates gratitude and excellence.
- Pray for divine timing before reaching out.
- Be ready to present your business, vision, or service with clarity, confidence, and humility.

Reflection Questions

1. Who are the "important people" God may be calling you to connect with in this season?

2. What gifts, skills, or seeds of honor can you offer that demonstrate excellence and generosity?

3. Are you willing to invest time, resources, and humility to learn from those who have gone before you?

4. How can you better prepare spiritually and professionally for divine connections?

PRAYER PROMPT

"Father, thank You for the gifts You've placed in me and for the divine connections You are aligning for my business and destiny. Lead me by Your Spirit to the right people and opportunities. Teach me to walk in generosity, wisdom, and honor. Help me to recognize when You are opening a door and to move with confidence and grace. May my gift make room for me, and may every connection bring You glory and expand the influence of Your Kingdom through my business.

In Jesus' name, Amen."

SCRIPTURE REFERENCES

"A man's gift maketh room for him, and bringeth him before great men."

—PROVERBS 18:16 (KJV)

"A man's gift [given in love or courtesy] makes room for him and brings him before great men."

—PROVERBS 18:16 (AMP)

"A gift opens the way and ushers the giver into the presence of the great."

—PROVERBS 18:16 (NIV)

SHE MEANS BUSINESS DECLARATION

- My gift makes room for me and opens doors where I will make the greatest Kingdom impact.

- God connects me to the right people, places, and opportunities for my business growth.

- Every seed I sow multiplies back to me in wisdom, influence, and prosperity.

HER DIVINE PARTNER

For thy Maker is thine husband; the LORD of hosts is his name; and thy Redeemer the Holy One of Israel; The God of the whole earth shall he be called..

—Isaiah 54:5 (KJV)

Devotional

Never forget who your true business partner is—**the Lord of Heaven and Earth, the Commander and Chief of Heaven's Armies**, your Maker, your covenant maker, your Husband. He has not only called you to build, but has committed Himself to never leave you nor forsake you, to prosper the work of your hands, and guide you in all your ways, giving you the desires of your heart. What a great partner in business. There is no one better than Him, the Lord of Host.

Look what Deut. 30:9 says, *"Then the Lord your God will make you most prosperous in all the work of your hands and in the fruit of your womb, the young of your livestock and the crops of your land. The Lord will again delight in you and make you prosperous, just as he delighted in your ancestors, 10if you obey the Lord your God and keep his commands and decrees that are written in this Book of the Law and turn to the Lord your God with all your heart and with all your soul."* Deut. 30:9 (NIV)

In the NLT it says, *"The Lord your God will then make you successful in everything you do. He will give you many children and numerous livestock, and he will cause your fields to produce abundant harvests, for the Lord will again delight in being good to you as he was to your ancestors. 10The Lord your God will delight in you if you obey his voice and keep the commands and decrees written in this Book of Instruction, and if you turn to the Lord your God with all your heart and soul."* Deut. 30:9 (NLT)

When God declares that He is your Maker and Husband, He is revealing His divine partnership with you in your business affairs and in your whole life—spirit, soul, and body. "He's not a silent partner; He is an active Commander who directs strategies, opens doors, and causes expansion on every side."

You are not alone in the marketplace. Heaven's resources, wisdom, and favor are backing you up. When you step into a new opportunity, you bring the presence of God with you. When you speak, His authority is released. When you plan, His hand directs.

In Him, there is no lack. His reward for your faith and obedience is freedom—freedom from financial struggle, emotional exhaustion, and fear of failure. He leads you out of scarcity into supernatural increase.

You are breaking forth to the right and to the left—expanding your reach, your influence, and your impact. The shame of past setbacks, missed opportunities, or failed ventures will no longer define you. This is your season of divine expansion and covenant prosperity.

God is saying to you today: "Fear not. I am your Husband, your Defender, your Provider. I have chosen you to build and to flourish."

"When you see God as your divine business partner, lack loses its power and prosperity becomes your covenant right. You are not building alone—Heaven is invested in your success."

— Dr. Margo Bush

FAITH ACTION

Spend time today recognizing God as your divine business partner.

- Dedicate your business plans, clients, and financial goals to Him in prayer.
- Declare that His wisdom guides your decisions and His favor opens new opportunities.
- Speak these confessions aloud.

REFLECTION QUESTIONS

1. Have I fully invited God to be the CEO and lead strategist of my business?
2. What areas of my life or business still reflect fear, lack, or limitation?
3. How can I align my business goals more intentionally with God's Word and His direction?
4. What "breaking forth" or expansion am I believing God for this season?

Prayer Prompt

"Father, thank You for being my Maker and my Husband — the One who directs my path in life and business. I trust You as my divine business partner and Provider. I surrender every plan, decision, and vision to Your leadership. Lead me into prosperity, expansion, and freedom from lack. Break forth through me to the right and to the left, that my business may reflect Your glory and abundance. I walk forward in faith, fearless and confident that You are for me and not against me.

In Jesus' name, Amen."

Scripture References

"For your Maker is your bridegroom, his name, God-of-the-Angel-Armies! Your Redeemer is The Holy One of Israel, known as God of the whole earth."

—Isaiah 54:5 (KJV)

"For your husband is your Maker, The Lord of hosts is His name; and your Redeemer is the Holy One of Israel, Who is called the God of the whole earth."

—Isaiah 54:5 (AMP)

"For your Maker is your husband— the Lord Almighty is his name— the Holy One of Israel is your Redeemer; he is called the God of all the earth."

—Isaiah 54:5 (NIV)

She Means Business Declaration

- God is my divine business partner and my source of prosperity.
- I break forth on every side—increase and expansion are my portion.
- Lack has no place in my life or business—take my authority and walk in prosperity.

- I am fearless, fruitful, and full of faith.

SHE IS EXQUISITE

> One of them was Lydia, a businesswoman from the city of Thyatira who was a dealer of exquisite purple cloth and a Jewish convert. While Paul shared the good news with her, God opened her heart to receive Paul's message.
>
> —ACTS 16:14 (NIV)

DEVOTIONAL

Lydia's story is short but packed with powerful lessons for women in business. She was a **businesswoman**, a dealer of exquisite purple cloth—a highly valued commodity in her time—and a woman of faith, a Jewish convert, open to God's direction.

Let's take a closer look at the **purple cloth Lydia dealt in**. Purple dye was extremely rare and expensive, made from the secretions of certain sea snails. Thousands of snails were needed to produce even a small amount of dye, and the labor to extract it and dye the fabric was painstaking and time-consuming. Only the wealthy or elite could afford garments of this color, making it a symbol of **royalty, power, and prestige**.

In many ways, Lydia's purple cloth mirrors the **Blood of Christ**. Just as the dye was rare, costly, and required great effort to produce, Jesus' sacrifice was precious, costly, and purposeful. He gave His life willingly, shedding His blood to purchase our freedom and clothe us with righteousness. The richness of the purple represents the **worth and value of His sacrifice**—a gift that is priceless, transformative, and eternal.

When Paul shared the good news with her, God opened her heart to receive the message. Lydia's openness led to transformation—not just in her spiritual life, but also in her business and her household. She didn't just hear the message; she acted. Acts 16:15 records that she and her household were baptized, and she invited Paul and his companions to stay in her home.

Here's the lesson for you as a woman in business: **God opens doors when hearts are open**. Lydia's business success wasn't the only thing that mattered—her willingness to respond to God's leading multiplied her influence and impact.

Too often, we rely only on our skills, networks, or strategies. But God wants to partner with you. He can open hearts, opportunities, and doors in your business that no human effort can achieve alone. Like Lydia, your **faith and responsiveness** can create pathways for divine favor and Kingdom impact. Openness to God's guidance is your greatest business strategy.

Ask yourself:

- Are you open to God's leading in your business today?

- Are there opportunities He's placing before you that require faith to step through?

When your heart is aligned with God's purposes, **your business becomes a platform for influence, blessing, and transformation**, just as Lydia's became.

Day 21 | She Is Exquisite

"When your heart is aligned with His purpose and your business is built through wisdom, you carry Kingdom impact and influence."

—Dr. Margo Bush

Faith Action

Today, take one step of faith in your business that aligns with God's leading. It could be a new connection, a bold idea, or an act of generosity. Write it down and pray over it, asking God to open the hearts of those you serve.

Reflection Questions

1. In what areas of your business do you need to be more open to God's guidance?

2. How does the value and rarity of Lydia's purple cloth inspire you to see your business and gifts as instruments of Kingdom impact?

3. What is one step you can take today to align your business with God's purpose?

Prayer Prompt

"Lord, thank You for the example of Lydia. Open my heart to Your guidance and direction in my business. Help me see the value You have placed in my gifts, my work, and my influence. Give me courage to step into the opportunities You are providing, and let my business be a blessing to those around me.

In Jesus' name, Amen."

SCRIPTURE REFERENCES

[5]Trust in the Lord completely, and do not rely on your own opinions. With all your heart rely on him to guide you, and he will lead you in every decision you make. [6] Become intimate with him in whatever you do, and he will lead you wherever you go.

—PROVERBS 3:5–6 (TPT)

For I know the plans I have for you…

—JEREMIAH 29:11 (KJV)

God shall supply all your need according to His riches in glory.

—PHILIPPIANS 4:19 (KJV)

You are a chosen people, a royal priesthood, a holy nation…

—1 PETER 2:9 (NIV)

SHE MEANS BUSINESS DECLARATION

- I am highly valued in my industry, and grow in business dealings and relationships.

- I am known in my industry as a woman of faith, integrity and grace.

- I work with integrity and diligence therefore God multiplies my influence and impact.

DAY 22

WOMAN OF WEALTH, WISDOM, AND THE WORD

No weapon that is formed against thee shall prosper; and every tongue that shall rise against thee in judgment thou shalt condemn. This is the heritage of the servants of the LORD, and their righteousness is of me, saith the LORD.

—Isaiah 54:17 (KJV)

Devotional

In early 2011, I took a trip to Zimbabwe in South Africa. What was meant to be a ministry trip quickly turned into a moment that tested my faith and courage. I was taken to the police station without explanation, surrounded by officers questioning my every move. I remember sitting there, heart pounding, feeling completely out of control—but not without hope.

The Lord reminded me of Isaiah 54:17: *"No weapon formed against thee shall prosper."* In that moment, I didn't just quote it—I lived it. I whispered it under my breath like a battle cry until peace filled that room. Within hours, I was released without harm, without charge, and without fear. God had already gone before me.

Starting, running, and growing a business requires that same kind of courage. It's not for the faint of heart. There will be moments when you feel surrounded—by financial pressure, critics, or unexpected setbacks. But the woman of God rises in authority, not anxiety. She knows that Heaven is invested in her success.

No weapon—no failed deal, no rejection, no betrayal—can prosper when your life and business are built on the Rock. You are not a victim of circumstance; victory is your covenant promise. God's promises are your defense strategy, and His Word is your legal right to prosper.

Every business faces battles: unexpected expenses, demanding clients, team conflict, or product failures. But wise businesswomen don't crumble—they *conquer*. Every trial becomes training. Every setback becomes a setup. Every storm builds new muscles of strength.

When I left that police station, I didn't walk out afraid—I walked out assured. God didn't just protect me; He promoted my faith. That same protection surrounds you in your business affairs. No weapon formed against your dreams or purpose will prosper, because your assignment is divine, your authority is spiritual, and your results are eternal.

"You are not building alone—Heaven is invested in your success."

—Dr. Margo Bush

Faith Action

Identify one challenge in your business right now. Instead of reacting in fear, respond in faith.

Pray for discernment and creative strategy. Then write down one bold action step that proves your trust in God even in adversity.

Reflection Questions

1. When have you seen God protect or promote you in an impossible situation?

2. What "weapons" (fear, doubt, lack, criticism) have tried to form against your success?

3. How can you use God's Word as your greatest defense and business strategy?

Prayer Prompt

"Heavenly Father, thank You that no weapon formed against me or my business will prosper. Strengthen my heart and mind to stand firm when opposition comes. Teach me to operate in divine wisdom, courage, and authority. Surround my business, my staff, and my clients with Your protection. Let every challenge become a testimony of Your faithfulness.

In Jesus' name, Amen."

Scripture References

"If God is for us, who can be against us?"

—Romans 8:31 (NIV)

"God sends angels with special orders to protect you wherever you go."

—Psalm 91:11 (TPT)

"The horse is prepared for the day of battle, but the victory belongs to the Lord."

—Proverbs 21:31 (NLT)

SHE MEANS BUSINESS DECLARATION

- I am a woman of wealth, wisdom, and the Word.

- No weapon formed against me, or my business shall prosper.

- I walk in divine favor, fueled by faith and fortified by Heaven.

- Every battle is a setup for a breakthrough, and every challenge pushes me closer to victory.

SHE KNOWS HOW TO PROSPER

> Beloved friend, I pray that you are prospering in every way and that you continually enjoy good health, just as your soul is prospering.
>
> —3 JOHN 1:2 (TPT)

DEVOTIONAL

I don't know what someone has told you about money, but here is the truth—**learning how to make money is a mindset**.

However you grew up and whatever you were told about money, has set your compass for how you view money. How money flows, how to make it, and how to keep it. I'll tell you right now—it's better to have money than not to have money. It's better to learn how to prosper than to live in a constant state of "barely getting by." It's better to live in overflow than to live on Barely-Get-Along Street. And you can have lots of money, and still have a **lack mindset**.

Yes, having wealth brings its own set of challenges—but so does *lack*. The difference is, God can give you the wisdom to handle abundance just as He's given you the grace to survive in scarcity.

I like to say it like this: There is a **Kingdom Wealth Code**, and it's perfectly suited for women who want to merge their love for God with their desire to grow a wildly successful business. Making a lot of money serving people is part of God's divine wealth principles—it focuses on the God-given design for prosperity.

Abraham is our father of faith, and he lived an extraordinarily abundant life. Solomon was so wise and rich that his life became our pattern for success throughout the book of Proverbs. John prayed for his beloved friends to prosper—and you can do the same: pray for your family to prosper, your friends to prosper, and your business to prosper.

God wants all of you—your spirit, soul, body, and finances—to thrive. You were **designed to prosper**. Deuteronomy 8:18 tells us that it is our covenant right and that He gives us the power to get wealth. *Claim it*!

There's a formula for success, just like there's a formula for staying poor. Prosperity doesn't happen by accident—it's learned, practiced, and stewarded.

If you've ever been told that money is evil, it's time to unlearn that lie. The Word of God says the **love of money** is the root of evil—not money itself. Money is a tool, and in the hands of Kingdom-minded women, it becomes a weapon for war—war against the devil.

Prosperity is a promise, and abundance is not optional—it's Biblical. Living below what God promised you is not humility—it's disobedience to the fullness of His Word. God is glorified when His daughters thrive, when we use our resources to bless others, serve our church, and when our success points back to His goodness.

The Formula for Success

There is a formula to success—and yes, it can be learned.

Think about it: every career has a process.

A doctor studies medicine.

A teacher studies education.

An engineer studies design and mathematics.

Success in those fields doesn't "just happen"—it's learned through knowledge, applied through discipline, and strengthened through consistency.

Business and prosperity are no different. There's a formula—a spiritual one and a practical one.

THE SPIRITUAL FORMULA

- **Faith:** Believe that prosperity is God's will for you.

- **Obedience:** Follow His voice, even when it stretches your comfort zone.

- **Sowing and Reaping:** Give generously, work diligently, and expect a return.

- **Gratitude:** Keep your heart humble and thankful for every blessing.

THE PRACTICAL FORMULA

- **Education:** Learn, learn, learn the systems that produce success—marketing, money management, leadership, and growth.

- **Execution:** Don't just learn— apply the plan.

- **Excellence:** Do everything with excellence—it attracts opportunity.

- **Endurance:** Stay diligent, determined, and driven.

Prosperity doesn't come by wishing—it comes by **wisdom**.

When you understand the spiritual laws that govern success and combine them with the practical laws of growth and business principles,

MEANS BUSINESS

your prosperity multiplies—and that glorifies God, not poverty, not lack, not scarcity.

Yes, you can learn how to become wildly successful, just like you can learn to be a brain surgeon, a nurse, or an astronaut. Prosperity isn't reserved for a lucky few—it's the right of every person who's willing to learn and apply principles of increase.

When you embrace that truth, you shift from surviving to thriving—and your life becomes a billboard for God's goodness.

"Prosperity isn't pride—it's partnership. When you walk in abundance, you become a living testimony that your Father is faithful."

—Dr. Margo Bush

Faith Action

Make a decision today to align your mindset with God's Word concerning prosperity. Write down three areas in your life or business where you want to see an increase—spiritually, financially, or physically—and begin praying and planning towards them. Create goals for your life and business. Set the date you will start (today) and the date you will accomplish them—a goal without a date is just a wish.

Reflection Questions

1. What early beliefs about money might still be limiting your financial growth?

2. Which area of your business or finances needs the most "tent-stretching" right now?

3. How can you honor God with greater excellence in your work this week?

Prayer Prompt

"Father, thank You for giving me the power to prosper. Teach me Your principles of increase and give me the wisdom to steward abundance well. I break every mindset of lack or fear that has kept me from walking in Your full abundance. I reject small thinking and embrace a Kingdom-mindset. Let my success be a testimony of Your goodness.

In Jesus' Name, Amen."

Scripture References

"Beloved, I wish above all things that thou mayest prosper and be in health, even as thy soul prospereth."

—3 John 1:2 (KJV)

"Dear friend, I pray that you may enjoy good health and that all may go well with you, even as your soul is getting along well."

—3 John 1:2 (NIV)

"Beloved, I pray that in every way you may succeed and prosper and be in good health [physically], just as [I know] your soul prospers [spiritually]."

—3 John 1:2 (AMP)

She Means Business Declaration

- I am a woman of wisdom, wealth, and the Word.
- I think big, act boldly, and live in overflow.
- I prosper in my spirit, soul, and body.

SHE BELIEVES AND SHE SPEAKS

> Put away from thee a froward mouth, and perverse lips put far from thee.
>
> —PROVERBS 4:24 (KJV)

DEVOTIONAL

In business and in life, your words set your course. They are not idle or insignificant—they are creative forces. Scripture reminds us that "death and life are in the power of the tongue" (Proverbs 18:21). What you say about your business, your future, and your abilities are shaping what you will walk into tomorrow.

As Kingdom entrepreneurs, we cannot afford to speak carelessly. Words of doubt, fear, or frustration tear down the very foundation we are trying to build. Proverbs 4:24 instructs us to *put away a froward mouth*—that means removing speech that contradicts what God has promised.

Instead, we must fill our mouths with faith-filled declarations—words that align with Heaven's truth about who we are and what we've been called to do. When you speak God's Word over your business, your voice becomes a weapon, sharper than any two-edged sword. Your confession cuts through limitation, opens doors of opportunity, and invites prosperity to manifest.

I've learned in my own entrepreneurial journey that what I spoke in faith during seasons of uncertainty eventually became my reality. As a young widow rebuilding my life and calling, I had to speak *before* I saw results. I declared success when circumstances looked small. I spoke expansively when my resources were limited. I confessed that God's favor surrounded me like a shield—and over time, I began to see exactly what I had spoken.

The Word says that if He calls you, He will equip you. That means you can speak with boldness and confidence because Heaven is backing every faith-filled word you release. Your mouth is the microphone of your faith—so turn up the volume and let your words agree with God's plan for your life and business.

Confession of a Woman Who Means Business

- I am a successful businesswoman, leader, and entrepreneur.

- My business makes $_____ a month.

- I am filled with wealth and wisdom to grow and market my business.

- Greatness is in Me!

- I was born for such a time as this. I am no accident; I am divinely positioned for prosperity.

- I am ready, prepared, and confident for this season in my life.

- I am a dynamic businesswoman and claim _____.

- I partner with God in everything I do in my business, and I will not grieve the Holy Spirit.

- His favor is on me; therefore, I am favored by others.

Day 24 | She Believes and She Speaks

- I am sought after in my industry.

"Faith speaks before it sees. When you speak with confidence and boldness, you give God something to move on."

—Dr. Margo Bush

Faith Action

- Identify one area of your business where you've been speaking doubt or frustration. Replace those words with Scripture-based declarations of faith and success.

- Confess daily who you already are, not going to be, or trying to be, but who the Word says you are over your business each morning.

- Write down three promises from God's Word that you can confess daily over your business growth, finances, and influence.

Reflection Questions

1. What words have you been speaking about your business that need to change today?

2. How can you intentionally use your voice to align with God's promises this week?

3. What does it look like for you to "speak boldly" in faith over your calling as an entrepreneur?

Prayer Prompt

"Lord, thank You for the power of life and death in my words! This means I have the power to speak into existence what God has already said I am: prosperous, whole, healed, anointed, born for greatness, appointed for such a time as this to serve people and fulfill my assignment. I will speak over my life and business in alignment with Your truth. Let every word I speak release favor, abundance, and confidence. Help me to guard my mouth from fear and negativity, and I intentionally fill it with declarations of faith and purpose. I believe it, I speak it, and I receive it.

In Jesus' name, Amen."

Scripture Reference

"Put away from you a deceitful mouth, and put perverse lips far from you."

—Proverbs 4:23 (NKJV)

"Keep your mouth free of perversity; keep corrupt talk far from your lips."

—Proverbs 4:23 (NIV)

"Put away from you a deceitful (lying, misleading) mouth, and put devious lips far from you."

—Proverbs 4:23 (AMP)

She Means Business Declaration

- I am generous, wise, and watch the words of my mouth, to speak only what the Word says about me.

- I declare that I will never do business alone. Jesus is my covenant business partner, my strategist, and my source.

- My purpose is God-ordained; my calling is unstoppable, and my life as an entrepreneur is a testimony of business success.

SHE IS A SUCCESSFUL BUSINESSWOMAN

She wraps herself in strength, might, and power in all her works. She tastes and experiences a better substance, and her shining light will not be extinguished, no matter how dark the night. She stretches out her hands to help the needy, and she lays hold of the wheels of government. She is known by all for her extravagant generosity to the poor, for she always reaches out her hands to those in need.

—Proverbs 31:17–18, 24 (TPT)

Devotional

The Proverbs 31 woman is often described as virtuous, but in today's language, we can also see her as a businesswoman and **Kingdom-minded entrepreneur**. She was industrious, wise, resourceful, and purposeful. She managed her home *and* operated her business. She sold goods, made strategic deals, and built influence that impacted her entire community.

Her work wasn't separate from her faith—it was her **faith in action**.

She didn't hustle for survival; she worked with divine strategy and purpose. Her entrepreneurial spirit flowed from her relationship with Him.

Proverbs 31:17 in the Amplified Bible says, *"She equips herself with strength [spiritual, mental, and physical fitness for her God-given task] and makes her arms strong."* She was fit—spiritually and mentally—to handle the weight of her assignment. She knew that her strength didn't come from striving but from her **connection to the Source** of all strength and success.

Colossians 3:23–24 (NIV) reminds us, *"Whatever you do, work at it with all your heart, as working for the Lord, not for human masters… It is the Lord Christ you are serving."*

This verse echoes the same truth: your work is your worship. When a woman of faith steps into her business, she's stepping into a God-given assignment. Her diligence, creativity, and excellence are spiritual expressions that bring Heaven's influence into the marketplace.

God anoints businesswomen with the ability to create wealth, not for self-gain, but for **Kingdom impact** (Deuteronomy 8:18). The Proverbs 31 woman used her skills to prosper—and her prosperity became a tool of generosity. Her lamp didn't go out because she understood stewardship and service.

As modern-day Kingdom entrepreneurs, we carry that same anointing. We are called to **prosper on purpose**—to build, serve, and lead with excellence so that others experience the goodness of God through our businesses. Your work matters to Heaven. Your business is ministry in motion. When you honor God with your gifts, your profit becomes prophetic—it declares that His blessing makes you rich and adds no sorrow.

So, equip yourself today with strength and vision. Wrap yourself in confidence and faith. You are anointed to prosper and appointed to make an impact.

Day 25 | She is a Successful Businesswoman

"Prosperity flows when your work becomes worship and your purpose becomes service."

—Dr. Margo Bush

Faith Action

- Dedicate your business to God today—acknowledge it as part of your divine assignment.
- List three ways your products, services, or leadership bless others and advance God's Kingdom.
- Pray for divine strength, strategy, and stamina to fulfill your marketplace calling with excellence.

Reflection Questions

1. How does viewing your business as a God-given assignment change your motivation and focus?
2. In what ways can you bring faith into your daily work decisions and interactions?
3. How can you use your business success to create greater Kingdom impact?

Confessions of Greatness, Prosperity, and Faith

- I am equipped and anointed for my Kingdom assignment in business.
- My work is worship; my business is ministry, and my success is impact.

- I prosper on purpose, creating wealth to advance God's Kingdom.

- I operate in wisdom, diligence, and divine strength.

- Everything I set my hands to do flourishes for God's glory.

PRAYER PROMPT

"Lord, thank You for the assignment You've placed on my life and in my business. Help me to see my work as holy and my efforts as worship. Strengthen my hands to build, serve, and prosper with excellence. Give me wisdom and creativity to expand with Kingdom purpose. Let my business shine as a light in the marketplace that glorifies You.

In Jesus' name, Amen."

SCRIPTURE REFERENCE

"She equips herself with strength [spiritual, mental, and physical fitness for her God-given task] and makes her arms strong…"

—PROVERBS 31:17–18, 24 (AMP)

"Whatever you do, work at it with all your heart…"

—COLOSSIANS 3:23–24 (NIV)

SHE MEANS BUSINESS DECLARATION

- I declare that wealth, wisdom, and divine strategy flow to me and through me.

- I operate in excellence, integrity, and supernatural intelligence.

- My decisions are Spirit-led, my hands are productive, and my work is prosperous.

Her Gift Opens Doors

Would you like to meet a very important person? Take a generous gift. It will do wonders to gain entrance into his presence.

—Proverbs 18:16 (TPT)

Devotional

Divine connections are one of the greatest catalysts for growth. God will often use relationships, meetings, and moments of favor to unlock the next level of your destiny. Proverbs 18:16 teaches us that **a generous gift opens doors**—not just physical doors, but doors of opportunity, influence, and wisdom.

A generous "gift" doesn't have to be a lot; it can also be your **skill, service, honor, or time**—something of value that you bring to the table. God designed your gifts to make room for you—to place you before people who can expand your knowledge, sharpen your business acumen, and elevate your vision.

As a businesswoman, become sensitive to divine timing and divine placement. There are **"very important people"** God has already positioned along your path—mentors, investors, clients, and teachers—who carry something you need to expand. Listen to God leading you into their presence and come prepared, both spiritually and professionally.

As the New Year of 2022 approached, I sought the Lord about the next steps for my life and business. I wanted a clear direction for how to expand and move forward. During that time, the Lord impressed upon my heart to begin attending a specific couples' ministry meeting every time they gathered in their hometown. I had been there before, but this time, I knew it was an instruction—a divine assignment.

So I obeyed. Month after month, I attended those meetings. In the natural, nothing remarkable seemed to be happening—no breakthroughs, no dramatic shifts—just powerful teaching and a consistent time in God's presence. But each time I went, I took a generous gift, sowing into the Word and honoring the prompting of the Holy Spirit. What I didn't realize then was that God was preparing the ground beneath my feet for a greater season of expansion.

By the end of the second year, the Lord began to speak clearly to me about my next assignment—and it was big. It was time to take the business to a new level, a level that required bold faith and divine confidence. Looking back, I see how every trip, every teaching, and every act of obedience positioned me for that moment. God was building capacity in me long before I saw the opportunity.

It pays to obey, even when you don't understand what the Lord is doing. Every step of obedience plants a seed for your next season. You may not see it right away, but God always sees ahead—and when the time is right, He reveals the purpose behind the preparation.

Generosity unlocks favor. Honor opens hearts. When you bring your best—not just what's convenient—you demonstrate the Kingdom principle of **seedtime and harvest**. Sometimes your best is—you. Your just showing up produces favor. When you sow your time, respect, and money, your return multiplies in influence and prosperity.

Don't be afraid to invest in relationships that stretch you. Attend that conference, reach out to that leader, enroll in that course, send that thoughtful gift or thank-you note. Each act of generosity becomes a bridge that God uses to connect you to the people who will help expand your business and sharpen your understanding of wealth and riches.

Seek the Lord's leading. He knows exactly who you need to meet, when you need to meet them, and how to prepare for that moment. Your gift will do wonders—not because of manipulation, but because of divine favor and obedience.

"Diligence is the bridge between vision and victory."

—Dr. Margo Bush

Faith Action

Ask God to highlight one "very important person" you need to connect with in this season—someone whose wisdom, experience, or influence can help you grow.

- Prepare a **seed of honor**—a gift, gesture, or message that communicates gratitude and excellence.

- Pray for divine timing before reaching out.

- Be ready to present your business, vision, or service with clarity, confidence, and humility.

Reflection Questions

1. Who are the "important people" God may be calling you to connect with in this season?

2. What gifts, skills, or seeds of honor can you offer that demonstrate excellence and generosity?

3. Are you willing to invest time, resources, and humility to learn from those who have gone before you?

4. How can you better prepare spiritually and professionally for divine connections?

PRAYER PROMPT

"Father, thank You for the gifts You've placed in me and for the divine connections You are aligning for my business, dreams, and destiny. Lead me by Your Spirit to the right people and opportunities. Teach me to walk in generosity, wisdom, and honor. Help me to recognize when You are opening a door and to move with confidence and grace. May my gift make room for me, and may every connection bring You glory and expand the influence of Your Kingdom through my business.

In Jesus' name, Amen."

SCRIPTURE REFERENCES

"A man's gift maketh room for him, and bringeth him before great men."

—PROVERBS 18:16 (KJV)

"A man's gift [given in love or courtesy] makes room for him and brings him before great men."

—PROVERBS 18:16 (AMP)

"A gift opens the way and ushers the giver into the presence of the great."

—PROVERBS 18:16 (NIV)

SHE MEANS BUSINESS DECLARATION

- My gift makes room for me and puts me in the room with the right people.

DAY 26 | HER GIFT OPENS DOORS

- I walk in divine favor and supernatural opportunities to do great things in business and in life.

- God connects me to the right people, places, and opportunities for my spiritual and business growth.

FOR SUCH A TIME AS THIS SHE LIVES

For if thou altogether holdest thy peace at this time, then shall there enlargement and deliverance arise to the Jews from another place; but thou and thy father's house shall be destroyed: and who knoweth whether thou art come to the kingdom for such a time as this?

—Esther 4:14 (KJV)

DEVOTIONAL

Most of us are familiar with the story of Esther, and this powerful verse in Esther 4:14. It has inspired movies, plays, and countless retellings, including *One Night with the King* (2006), where a young Jewish woman hides her origins while the Persian king searches for a bride.

But for today's devotional, let's step back to Esther 4:3 and focus on Mordecai, her uncle and guardian. His faith and courage in the face of danger are lessons every businesswoman can learn from:

> *"And Mordecai told them to answer Esther: 'Do not think in your heart that you will escape in the king's palace any*

> *more than all the other Jews. For if you remain completely silent at this time, relief and deliverance will arise for the Jews from another place…'"*
>
> —Esther 4:13-14a (NKJV)

Notice this: Mordecai gave Esther a choice. She could obey God and step into the divine purpose for which He had positioned her—or remain silent and safe. God had placed her in the palace for such a time as this.

The same is true for you as a woman in business: God has positioned you where you are for a divine assignment. He has given you gifts, vision, and opportunities, but obedience is required to see them fulfilled.

Perhaps you've had ideas, dreams, or business opportunities that seemed too risky, too hard or too scary. Fear, self-doubt, or timing may have held you back. Verse 14 reminds us:

> *"If you remain completely silent at this time, relief and deliverance will arise from another place…"*

God's work will still be accomplished—with you or without you. But when you step forward in obedience, you become the vessel of His blessings and provision. Acting on God's guidance moves you into prosperity, fulfillment, and a destiny uniquely yours.

Ask yourself: What is God calling me to do today? What dream, idea, or business opportunity has He placed in my heart that I've ignored? Your obedience opens doors for deliverance, influence, and Kingdom impact.

> *"When God positions you, it's never random—He's aligning you for divine impact."*
>
> —Dr. Margo Bush

FAITH ACTION

Take a moment today to write down one action God is calling you to take in your business or career. It may feel scary or impossible—but commit to obeying Him, even in small steps, and watch Him open doors that only His favor can unlock.

REFLECTION QUESTIONS

1. What is one area in your business or life where you've remained silent instead of stepping out in faith?

2. How would your approach change if you trusted that God positioned you exactly "for such a time as this"?

3. What fear or excuse has been holding you back from acting on God's calling in your life?

PRAYER PROMPT

"Lord, thank You for placing me exactly where I am for such a time as this. Give me courage to obey Your calling, to act on the dreams and opportunities You've placed in my heart. Remove fear and self-doubt, and help me step boldly into the purpose and prosperity You have for me.

In Jesus' name, Amen."

SCRIPTURE REFERENCES

"[5] Trust in the Lord completely, and do not rely on your own opinions. With all your heart rely on him to guide you, and he will lead you in every decision you make. [6] Become intimate with him in whatever you do, and he will lead you wherever you go."

—PROVERBS 3:5–6 (TPT)

"Before I formed you in the womb, I knew you."

—Jeremiah 1:5 (KJV)

"I press toward the mark of the high calling of God."

—Philippians 3:14 (KJV)

"Commit thy way unto the Lord; trust also in Him, and He shall bring it to pass."

—Psalm 37:5 (KJV)

She Means Business Declaration

- I declare I was born for such a time as this to fulfill the assignment on my life.

- I was born at this time, right on time, to use my gifts and talents to create Kingdom impact.

- I declare that I am mighty like an army—full of power, valor, and victory.

- No assignment is too great, no obstacle too strong, and no battle too fierce, because the Lord is my strength, my partner, and my defender.

DAY 28

SHE IS LEADING IN THE MARKETPLACE

> I don't depend on my own strength to accomplish this; however, I do have one compelling focus: I forget all of the past as I fasten my heart to the future instead.
>
> —PHILIPPIANS 3:13 (TPT)

DEVOTIONAL

"I don't depend on my own strength to accomplish this."

What a freeing statement for every woman in business!

When you try to build your business or pursue your marketplace calling solely in your own wisdom and strength, it becomes exhausting—spiritually, mentally, and physically. You were never meant to carry that weight alone—you were never meant to **Do Business Alone**. You have the ultimate business partner—**Jesus Christ**—who gives you success, strategy, and strength for every season. There is a supernatural supply that only He can bring and it is so much better than all we can do on our own. He opens doors where doors are closed. He provides clients when there seems to be no supply. He negotiates contracts when you have come to the end of all talks.

> *"Act like it all depends on you and believe like it all depends on God."*
>
> —Mark Batterson
> Pastor and Author of The Circle Maker

He knows the plans He has for you. He knew your name before anyone else did. As Jeremiah reminds us, *"Before I formed you in your mother's womb, I knew you."* (Jeremiah 1:5) No matter your past—whether you were planned, unplanned, adopted, or left to figure things out on your own—God personally crafted you for a divine assignment. Every challenge, every opportunity, every season is shaping you for divine destiny.

> *"And who knows but that God has placed you in the royal palace for just such a time as this?"*
>
> —Esther 4:14 (TPT)

The King James translation says, *"For if thou altogether holdest thy peace at this time, then shall there enlargement and deliverance arise to the Jews from another place; but thou and thy father's house shall be destroyed: and who knoweth whether thou art come to the kingdom for such a time as this?"*

You're not too late, too young, too old, or too far gone. The phrase *"for such a time as this"* highlights divine timing and purpose—God's intentional placement of Esther (and you) to fulfill a specific purpose at the exact right moment in time. The same God who called Esther into her divine assignment has positioned you in your business, career, ministry, or marketplace to fulfill a divine purpose. You were approved, anointed, and appointed to walk this journey of divine assignment on your life.

Stop striving in your own strength and start partnering with the One who never fails and never runs out of ideas or clients. He will guide you in all of your business decisions if you will take the time to ask Him. Ask Him to open new doors, to lead you into wisdom and wealth. When your dream feels bigger than you, then you know you are right on track.

DAY 28 | SHE IS LEADING IN THE MARKETPLACE

Esther had a bigger assignment than she could do on her own. It took faith instead of fear, obedience instead of opposition, and strategy instead of stubbornness.

Paul said:

> *"I press toward the mark for the prize of the high calling of God in Christ Jesus."*
>
> —PHILIPPIANS 3:14 (KJV)

"Well done, thou good and faithful servant," is our prize. When you can say, *"I've done all that God has asked me to do,"* then you can go home and be with the Lord. Until then, get busy fulfilling your dreams and following His assignment on your life.

Jesus will be the author and finisher of your faith—go with Him. Your assignment is not done yet. You still have some business to do with God. Whether you are in ministry or in the marketplace, your calling to help people is no less than someone standing in the pulpit. Your pulpit is the marketplace. Your service is to people. The product(s) you offer are meant to make someone's life more successful and easier.

Press toward the mark for the prize of the high calling, be found faithful doing what God has assigned you to do. **Mark my word:** if you press toward that mark—it will lead to divine destiny.

"God never called you to do business alone—He called you to partner with Heaven and follow His wisdom."

—DR. MARGO BUSH

FAITH ACTION

Pause and speak over your business today, what the Word says you are and have. Ask God to show you areas where you've been striving in your own strength and not relying on Him to work on your behalf—

behind the scenes. Release worry to Him today and invite the Holy Spirit to direct your path, guide you into the right places, to meet the right people, to make the right calls. Claim His wisdom, favor, and believe in His timing to work all things for your good and prosperity.

REFLECTION QUESTIONS

1. What specific part of your business or calling have you been trying to handle without God's help?

2. How can you begin inviting Him into your daily decision-making?

3. What does "pressing toward the mark" look like for you right now in your business or leadership journey?

PRAYER PROMPT

"Heavenly Father, thank You for being my ultimate business partner. I choose today to stop striving and start trusting. Teach me to lead with Your strength, not my own. Open new doors of wisdom, favor, and divine strategy. Like Esther, I want to fulfill my purpose "for such a time as this." I press toward the mark, knowing that You will finish what You started in me.

In Jesus' name, Amen."

SCRIPTURE REFERENCES

"Brethren, I do not count myself to have apprehended; but one thing I do, forgetting those things which are behind and reaching forward to those things which are ahead, 14 I press toward the goal for the prize of the upward call of God in Christ Jesus."

—PHILIPPIANS 3:13–14

"Before I formed you in the womb I knew you; Before you were born I sanctified you; I ordained you a prophet to the nations."

—Jeremiah 1:5

"For if you remain completely silent at this time, relief and deliverance will arise for the Jews from another place, but you and your father's house will perish. Yet who knows whether you have come to the kingdom for such a time as this?"

—Esther 4:14

"Commit your works to the Lord, And your thoughts will be established."

—Proverbs 16:3

"And let us not grow weary while doing good, for in due season we shall reap if we do not lose heart."

—Galatians 6:9

SHE MEANS BUSINESS DECLARATION

- I am anointed and appointed for such a time as this.
- I do not strive in my own strength—I partner with Heaven.
- I lead with divine strategy, wisdom, and courage.

SHE MASTERS HER TIME

Help us to remember that our days are numbered, and help us to interpret our lives correctly. Set your wisdom deeply in our hearts so that we may accept your correction.

—PSALM 90:12 (TPT)

DEVOTIONAL

What are you doing with the 24 hours you've been given?

How are you investing the time God has entrusted to you?

Every woman—whether a billionaire in her mansion, a student in her dorm room, or a mother raising her children—has one equal gift from Heaven: **time**. How we use it, steward it, and master it determines the outcome of our future.

Time is Heaven's democratic gift.

No one gets more. No one gets less.

The difference between success and stagnation is stewardship of time.

Every hour wasted is a piece of your destiny delayed.

Moses prayed in Psalm 90, *"Help us to remember that our days are numbered…"* He continues, *"Set Your wisdom deeply in our hearts so that we may accept Your correction."*

I like to say it like this:

> **"Lord, set Your wisdom deep in my heart so I may accept Your correction and know Your direction."**

You cannot continue walking your own path, using time however you want, and expect to fulfill your divine purpose. God's correction keeps you aligned with His direction—and His direction leads you straight into success, clarity, and calling.

Recently, I met a beautiful young woman from China who came to America to chase the "American Dream." Her success was obvious—wealth surrounded her home. Yet inside, her heart was empty. Her soul was aching. Why? Because you cannot spend all your time building success while ignoring the One who created you for fellowship.

Time is the opportunity you've been given to draw closer to God, pursue your divine purpose, and make a Kingdom impact.

Time is the currency of destiny.

How you steward your time is how you steward your life.

If your hours are spent scrolling, binge-watching, or in distraction—yet your finances are in shambles, your business is stagnant, and your client list is empty—something must change.

Life doesn't get better by chance; it gets better by *change*.

Jesus modeled this for us. He spent time with the Father **first**—before decisions, before ministry, before the crowds. If you misuse your mornings, you'll misuse your miracles.

Have you sought His direction today?

Have you asked for His counsel, His wisdom, His strategies?

Mastering your time is mastering your life.

Daniel understood this.

> *"He kneeled upon his knees three times a day, and prayed…"*
>
> —Daniel 6:10–11

He scheduled his prayer life like an unbreakable appointment.

That discipline produced the spirit of excellence that promoted him.

Paul understood it too:

He disciplined his time, mastered his thoughts, and conquered his emotions.

That's how he wrote over half the New Testament.

> *"[24]Isn't it obvious that all runners on the racetrack keep on running to win, but only one receives the victor's prize? Yet each one of you must run the race to be victorious. [25] A true athlete will be disciplined in every respect, practicing constant self-control in order to win a laurel wreath that quickly withers. But we run our race to win a victor's crown that will last forever. [26] For that reason, I don't run just for exercise or box like one throwing aimless punches, [27] but I train like a champion athlete. I subdue my body and get it under my control, so that after preaching the good news to others, I myself won't be disqualified."*
>
> —1 Corinthians 9:24-27 (TPT)

Athletes have strict training and routines. They rise early, train when they are tired, resist the temptation to quit, and endure discomfort—because they stay focused—on the prize. When your focus is broken, your business will be broke. Champions do what it takes to win, while others are losing at life.

If you want champion-level success in business, you must develop champion-level mastery.

How to Master Your Time

1. **Focus**

   Stay focused on winning. Champions don't talk about quitting. Take every thought of defeat captive.

2. **Discipline**

   Train your body and your emotions to obey your assignment. Winners don't train like amateurs—they train like champions.

3. **Consistency**

   Practice self-control daily. Subdue your body, discipline your mind, command your focus. Don't let your feelings lead—*you* lead them.

When you master your focus, you'll control your future.

When you steward your time, you'll steward your wealth.

When you control consistency, you'll increase your currency.

Stop saying you don't have enough time. The only thing that is different between those who have more and those who don't is how they have chosen to spend the 24 hours in their day.

You want success? Spend each hour on actions that create success. Value each hour like a champion athlete values each workout and training. Like, there is a prize at the end of the day—because there is. Stop scrolling and practice self-control. Stop complaining and become consistent. Stop the destructive talk and be disciplined.

"Time is the currency of destiny—spend it with intention, and you'll master your wealth."

—Dr. Margo Bush

Faith Action

Choose one area of your day that wastes the most time. Remove it. Replace it with 30 minutes of prayer, learning, or focused action towards business success.

Reflection Questions

1. What is the biggest "time thief" in your daily routine?

2. How would your business change if you stewarded your mornings with intention?

3. What is one discipline you can start today to increase your productivity?

Prayer Prompt

"Lord, teach me to number my days with wisdom. Help me steward my time with discipline and focus. Redirect every wasted hour and realign my heart with Your purpose. Strengthen me to master my habits, emotions, and daily decisions so I may walk boldly in my assignment.

In Jesus' name, Amen."

Scripture References

"So teach us to number our days, That we may gain a heart of wisdom."

—Psalm 90:12

"10 Now when Daniel knew that the writing was signed, he went home. And in his upper room, with his windows open toward Jerusalem, he knelt down on his knees three times that day, and prayed and gave thanks before his God, as was his custom since early days.

11 Then these men assembled and found Daniel praying and making supplication before his God."

—Daniel 6:10–11

"[24]Isn't it obvious that all runners on the racetrack keep on running to win, but only one receives the victor's prize? Yet each one of you must run the race to be victorious. [25] A true athlete will be disciplined in every respect, practicing constant self-control in order to win a laurel wreath that quickly withers. But we run our race to win a victor's crown that will last forever. [26] For that reason, I don't run just for exercise or box like one throwing aimless punches, [27] but I train like a champion athlete. I subdue my body and get it under my control, so that after preaching the good news to others I myself won't be disqualified."

—1 Corinthians 9:24–27 (TPT)

"But seek first the kingdom of God and His righteousness, and all these things shall be added to you."

—Matthew 6:33

Day 29 | She Masters Her Time

"Now in the morning, having risen a long while before daylight, He went out and departed to a solitary place; and there He prayed."

—Mark 1:35

She Means Business Declaration

- I am a woman who masters her time.

- I rise with purpose, steward my hours with wisdom, and walk in divine focus.

- My time is aligned with Heaven, and my life produces excellence, increase, and impact.

HER MISSION IN THE MARKETPLACE

I press toward the mark for the prize of the high calling of God in Christ Jesus.

—Philippians 3:14 (KJV)

DEVOTIONAL

Your business journey is not just about building a successful company—it's also about fulfilling the high calling God has placed on your life—your mission in the marketplace.

I was a pastor's wife for twenty-eight years until my husband suddenly died. A year before his passing, I woke up one morning with Jesus standing by my bed. When I saw Him, I immediately left my body. The next thing I knew, I was standing on the edge of a building ledge with Jesus, looking out over the city. Across the street, I saw a set of high-rise buildings, but one particularly stood out to me. It was an eight-story building divided into two sections—four stories on the bottom and four stories on the top.

There was a group of people on the bottom four floors whom I recognized. I asked Jesus, *"Who are they, Lord? Why are they all there?"* He said, *"Those are all the people I sent you to. They are out doing the will of My Father because you obeyed My call to go pastor in the place I called you."* I then asked, *"Who are all those people in the top four floors?"* They were different from the ones below—a group of businessmen and women at an event or party. Some had cocktails in their hands. Most of the men were wearing suits, and the women were dressed in corporate casual attire. Jesus said to me, *"Those are all the ones I am now sending you to—and if you will go, they will come to know Me."*

As Jesus finished that sentence, He was suddenly gone and I turned to find a pair of pink tennis shoes in the middle of the floor. I ran over and began to put them on. As I did, I was back in my body and heard myself gasp for air before I was gone again.

This time, I was on a dirt road. Jesus was on my left and Bill (my husband) was on my right as we walked down a country dirt road. Soon, we came to a fork in the road, and Bill turned to walk down the road on the right while Jesus and I turned left down the road. I began to cry out to Bill, *"Please don't leave me! I don't want to walk this road by myself! Please, please don't leave me!"* The powerful presence of Jesus walking beside me kept me moving forward with Him, though I kept turning and calling after Bill.

Then Bill turned around, and with a calm, confident, peaceful voice, he said, *"I have finished my race. I have done everything that the Lord has asked me to do, and I have won my reward. But your race is not finished yet—you have more to do. Go with Jesus; He will be the author and finisher of your faith."* As he spoke those words, Jesus' steady walk ahead turned my body forward, as though we were on an escalator. That was the last thing I heard from Bill before I returned to my body—wide awake in my bed.

Jesus talked to me about many things that day, but I have never seen Him like that again. One year later, almost to the day, Bill went home to be with the Lord. He finished his race here on earth—I was forty-nine.

Philippians 3:14 encourages us to press forward, stay focused, and persevere toward the prize that God has set before us. Your destiny was already planned in the heart of God before you were ever born. He knew you when He formed you in your mother's womb. God's plan for your life—whether you are called to the marketplace or ministry—is a divine call to serve and minister to people.

If you're in bookkeeping, you're helping people with their financial future. If you're a cook or own a restaurant, you're feeding the hungry. If you're a coach, teacher, or professor, you're empowering people to grow and become all God has called them to be. If you're a manager, executive, leader, speaker, politician, or surgeon—you are a *sent one* into that industry to impact it for the Kingdom of God.

This verse reminds us that success is more than achievements or accolades—it's about divine destiny. You were handpicked by God to do what you do, to influence your industry, to be in that place for *such a time as this*. You are not there by chance; you are divinely appointed by the Creator to walk in His purpose.

> *"For if thou altogether holdest thy peace at this time, then shall there enlargement and deliverance arise to the Jews from another place; but thou and thy father's house shall be destroyed: and who knoweth whether thou art come to the kingdom for such a time as this?"*
>
> —Esther 4:14 (KJV)

Are you where you are because *thou art come to the kingdom for such a time as this*? Every ethical decision, every step of diligent work, every faithful act in your business, every action of love for family or church, contributes to the fulfillment of your high calling. Challenges and setbacks may arise, but the call remains the same—to press forward despite circumstances, trusting God and committing your ways to Him.

Matthew 25:21 affirms:

"Well done, thou good and faithful servant: thou hast been faithful over a few things, I will make thee ruler over many things: enter thou into the joy of thy lord."

When we stand before Jesus, we will give an account of all we have done for Him. I want to hear those words: *"Well done, thou good and faithful servant."* I have committed my life to fulfill all that God has

MEANS BUSINESS

called me to do in the marketplace and in ministry. I don't want to go to my grave with anything left undone, that God had on His agenda for me.

Don't get me wrong—I'm not perfect. I can be slow to obey. But somehow, I find the courage to get back on that dirt road and walk alongside Jesus. It's a much better place to be.

Pressing toward the prize means setting your eyes on God's purpose, not temporary comfort or fleeting success. It's a daily commitment to take bold, faithful steps, knowing that one day you will hear, *"Well done, good and faithful servant."*

Your faithfulness today shapes the Kingdom impact you will make and the prosperity you will hold.

"Step boldly, serve faithfully, shine relentlessly—your marketplace mission carries Heaven's assignment."

—Dr. Margo Bush

Faith Action

Take time today to reaffirm your calling in the marketplace. Write out how your work serves God's Kingdom. Ask the Holy Spirit to show you one way you can impact your sphere of influence for His glory this week.

Reflection Questions

1. How does your current work reflect your Kingdom purpose?

2. Have you been faithful in the assignment God has already given you?

3. What practical steps can you take to ensure your business reflects God's excellence and integrity?

Prayer Prompt

"Father, thank You for calling me to serve You in the marketplace. Strengthen my hands to work with diligence and faith. Help me to stay focused on the high calling You've placed on my life. Give me wisdom, courage, and grace to press forward and complete my assignment with excellence.

In Jesus' Name, Amen."

Scripture References

"I press toward the mark for the prize of the high calling of God in Christ Jesus."

—Philippians 3:14 (KJV)

"For if thou altogether holdest thy peace at this time, then shall there enlargement and deliverance arise to the Jews from another place; but thou and thy father's house shall be destroyed: and who knoweth whether thou art come to the kingdom for such a time as this?"

—Esther 4:14 (KJV)

"His lord said unto him, Well done, thou good and faithful servant: thou hast been faithful over a few things, I will make thee ruler over many things: enter thou into the joy of thy lord."

—Matthew 25:21 (KJV)

"Before I formed thee in the belly I knew thee; and before thou camest forth out of the womb I sanctified thee, and I ordained thee a prophet unto the nations."

—Jeremiah 1:5 (KJV)

SHE MEANS BUSINESS DECLARATION

- I am called, chosen, and commissioned for such a time as this.

- My business is my ministry, my marketplace is my mission field, and my obedience is my offering.

- I press toward the mark of my high calling in Christ Jesus, and I will finish my race with joy—faithful, fruitful, and full of purpose.

DAY 31

SHE MEANS BUSINESS

> Who could ever find a wife like this one—she is a woman of strength and mighty valor! She's full of wealth and wisdom. The price paid for her was greater than many jewels.
>
> —Proverbs 31:10 (TPT)

Devotional

The Hebrew word used to describe this virtuous wife is ***"khayil."*** There is no English word that fully captures its meaning: **military strength**—implying might, valor, and victory. This word is often used in connection **with military prowess**.

This woman is not timid or passive. She is a **warring wife**—strong in spirit, morally righteous, excellent, wealthy, full of substance, integrity, abilities, and strength; mighty like an army.

Let's look at how various translations ask this question in Proverbs 31:10:

- *"Who can find a virtuous woman?" (KJV)*

- *"An excellent woman [one who is spiritual, capable, intelligent, and virtuous]—who is he who can find her?" (AMP)*

- *"A good woman is hard to find, and worth far more than diamonds." (MSG)*

- *"A wife of noble character who can find? She is worth far more than rubies." (NIV)*

Isn't that a beautiful picture of who God calls you to be? You are the virtuous woman, the Proverbs 31 woman He has paid for. You're not trying to become a virtuous woman; the Lord is speaking over you, who you already are.

That word *greater* in Hebrew denoted **her worth**—a worth purchased by the **sacred Blood of the Lamb of God**, her Bridegroom. You were bought with a price no man can touch. You are worth more than rubies (to Him), more than diamonds, more than any physical product on earth is worth. The entire chapter of Proverbs 31 talks about who you are and who He has made you—not who you are 'not' and need to become. That sacred Blood of Christ bought for you a covenant that **speaks. He is speaking over you—Woman of Wealth and Wisdom, Strength and Mighty Warrior. You're not trying to become this woman; you are who He says you are.**

As a new bride, getting ready to meet your Bridegroom, as you enter through those church sanctuary doors to walk down the aisle to say those very important two words, 'I do,' you take on everything that your new husband is and has. His name, his riches, his debt, his children, his family—everything. You become 'One Flesh' in the eyes of your friends and family, the court's, and the Lord.

After the untimely death of my husband—my lover, best friend, a great father, and faithful pastor—I was heartbroken and felt alone for the first time in my life. We had been in full-time ministry from the day we said, "I do." Together we pastored churches, ministered throughout the US, and taught in Churches and Bible Schools around the world. We worked in our businesses together, but I had never run a successful business on my own before, yet God said to me,

"Take this publishing house and grow it. I will be your business partner, and together we will grow it."

I hate to admit this, but there were months when I didn't let Him be my partner. I tried to handle things on my own—until desperation drove me to surrender. Too often, we wait until all else fails before talking to the Master business builder, the One who knows all things and cares about our success more than anyone else ever could.

He wants us to succeed even more than we want to. He wants us to *fulfill* our dreams more than we want to. He is working on our behalf, even when we don't think anything is going on. He's behind the scenes, for our success. We have a covenant with Him—so we are not trying to become this successful businesswoman. He is already calling us a virtuous woman worth more than rubies—**khayil:** *mighty, wealthy, excellent, morally righteous, full of substance, integrity, abilities and strength, mighty like an army.*

How to Be a Proverbs 31 Woman

1. **Agree with God.**

   Proverbs 31 is not just a description—it's a confession. Speak it over yourself daily as your divine identity.

2. **Ask Him to reveal to you His covenant promises.**

   Deuteronomy 8:18 promises, "It is He who gives you power to get wealth." Invite Him to guide your business decisions and show you the path to wealth and riches.

3. **Act in faith in the Word—no matter how you feel.**

   Don't allow fear, emotions, or limited thinking to hold you back from what Jesus has already paid for you. Your breakthrough is on the other side of obedience to His Word.

In 2009, I asked the Lord to send me a business coach. I had no money—a mountain of debt from a very expensive funeral bill, no life insurance policy—but God answered. Suddenly, out of nowhere, two weeks after that desperate prayer, a businessman called to offer me a job opening for Him on stage during his national business conferences.

How good is God to pay me for what I needed to learn, instead of me paying? Even through my grief, I believed God would supply abundantly. I didn't know how, but He always pays — He has never left me without.

Why? Because I took **Deuteronomy 8:18 and 3 John 2** literally:

> *"But thou shalt remember the LORD thy God: for it is he that **giveth thee power** to get wealth, that he may establish his covenant…"*
>
> —Deuteronomy 8:18 (KJV)

> *"Beloved, I pray that in every way you may succeed and prosper and be in good health [physically], just as [I know] your soul prospers [spiritually]."*
>
> —3 John 2 (MSG)

> *"Therefore I say unto you, What things soever ye desire, when ye pray, believe that ye receive **them**, and ye shall have **them**."*
>
> —Mark 11:24 (KJV)

Take Him at His Word and begin to speak this virtuous woman's poetic promise over your life and business as a confession of faith. Your dreams and visions are important to Him–He says you can and you are. Declare it. Do it. Dominate it, and watch what will begin to happen for you. As you pursue your purpose, He has already been calling you—*khayil*.

> *"You're not striving to become the Proverbs 31 woman you already are— a woman of virtue and valor, wealth and wisdom, filled with purpose and prosperity."*
>
> —Dr. Margo Bush

DAY 31 | SHE MEANS BUSINESS

FAITH ACTION

Write out Proverbs 31:10–31 in your journal and personalize each verse. Replace "she" and "her" with your name. Declare it daily. Example— *[your name] is a woman of strength and mighty valor, full of wealth and wisdom.*

REFLECTION QUESTIONS

1. In what areas have you tried to run your life or business without letting God be your partner?

2. What does Proverbs 31 mean to you personally?

3. What step of faith is God asking you to take today toward your own prosperity?

PRAYER PROMPT

"Heavenly Father, create in me a clean heart, O God—a woman of virtue and valor. Thank You for making me a woman of strength and might like an army, worthy of Your blood and full of wisdom. A businesswoman full of grace and love toward all mankind. Teach me to depend fully on You as my divine business partner—making me strong and confident in the boardroom. I seek Your wisdom to lead and grow what You have assigned me to do on this earth. Teach me how to better take hold of my covenant rights with honor and humility, reclaiming all that the enemy has stolen. I take my seat at the table and dine with You boldly and humbly, knowing that every good and perfect gift comes down from the Father of Lights. Everything I have flows from Your hand of favor and mercy. You are establishing Your covenant of wealth and prosperity in my life so that everything I do brings glory to Your name.

In Jesus' name, Amen."

SCRIPTURE REFERENCES

10 Who can find a virtuous woman? for her price is far above rubies.

 MEANS BUSINESS

11 The heart of her husband doth safely trust in her, so that he shall have no need of spoil.

12 She will do him good and not evil all the days of her life.

13 She seeketh wool, and flax, and worketh willingly with her hands.

14 She is like the merchants' ships; she bringeth her food from afar.

15 She riseth also while it is yet night, and giveth meat to her household, and a portion to her maidens.

16 She considereth a field, and buyeth it: with the fruit of her hands she planteth a vineyard.

17 She girdeth her loins with strength, and strengtheneth her arms.

18 She perceiveth that her merchandise is good: her candle goeth not out by night.

19 She layeth her hands to the spindle, and her hands hold the distaff.

20 She stretcheth out her hand to the poor; yea, she reacheth forth her hands to the needy.

21 She is not afraid of the snow for her household: for all her household are clothed with scarlet.

22 She maketh herself coverings of tapestry; her clothing is silk and purple.

23 Her husband is known in the gates, when he sitteth among the elders of the land.

24 She maketh fine linen, and selleth it; and delivereth girdles unto the merchant.

25 Strength and honour are her clothing; and she shall rejoice in time to come.

26 She openeth her mouth with wisdom; and in her tongue is the law of kindness.

27 She looketh well to the ways of her household, and eateth not the bread of idleness.

28 Her children arise up, and call her blessed; her husband also, and he praiseth her.

29 Many daughters have done virtuously, but thou excellest them all.

30 Favour is deceitful, and beauty is vain: but a woman that feareth the Lord, she shall be praised.

31 Give her of the fruit of her hands; and let her own works praise her in the gates.

—Proverbs 31:10–31 (KJV)

(Also see Proverbs 31:10-31 in AMP, TPT)

"But thou shalt remember the Lord thy God: for it is he that giveth thee power to get wealth, that he may establish his covenant which he sware unto thy fathers, as it is this day."

—Deuteronomy 8:18 (KJV)

"For ye are bought with a price: therefore glorify God in your body, and in your spirit, which are God's."

—1 Corinthians 6:20

"Thus saith the Lord, thy Redeemer, the Holy One of Israel; I am the Lord thy God which teacheth thee to profit, which leadeth thee by the way that thou shouldest go."

—Isaiah 48:17

> *"But my God shall supply all your need according to his riches in glory by Christ Jesus."*
>
> —Philippians 4:19

She Means Business Declarations

- I declare that I am a Proverbs 31 woman—strong, capable, valuable, and equipped.

- I am worth more than rubies because I am blood-bought, heaven-backed, and covenant-covered.

- I walk in confidence knowing I already AM the woman God says I am.

Congratulations!

You've completed 31 days of faith-building, increase, and prosperity-focused devotionals.

Remember: Growing a business that creates wealth is 90% mindset. What you believe about increase and prosperity is a battle in your mind that will make you, or break you. God has blessed your business, home, finances, and life. His promises are for you, and they are the absolute truth. His power works in you to will and do of His GOOD pleasure. It is your covenant right. Keep applying what you've learned:

- Trust God daily
- Act in faith
- Lead with integrity and love
- Give generously
- Seek His Kingdom first

Your business is more than a livelihood—it is a ministry, a platform, and a vehicle for influence. Stay faithful, persistent, and expect God's supernatural provision, protection, and favor to continue multiplying in your life.

This is my prayer over you—that you will see how extraordinary you are and that you have the ability to earn more, create financial security, and build for Kingdom-impact.

> *"Beloved, I pray that you may prosper in all things and be in health, just as your soul prospers."*
>
> —3 John 2

I believe you have it in you to grow a wildly successful business if you want one. God has designed you for prosperity and abundance.

I'm cheering you on,

−Dr. Margo Bush

SHE WALKS IN GREAT BLESSING

> Great blessing and wealth fills the house of the wise, for their integrity endures forever.
>
> —PSALM 112:3 (TPT)

DEVOTIONAL

"Great blessing and wealth fills the house of the wise…"

The Message Translation says, "Their **houses** brim with wealth."

The New International Version says, "Wealth and riches are in their **houses**."

Notice it says **houses** in both translations. That's real estate, income, and wealth building.

Second, it says **GREAT blessing and wealth fills the house...** That word **great** means: notably large in size; huge; elaborate; ample; remarkable in magnitude, degree, or effectiveness.

Why…does great blessing and wealth fill the house? Because of wisdom.

Psalm 112:1 tells us why:

> *"Praise ye the LORD. Blessed is the man that feareth the LORD, that delighteth greatly in his commandments."*

When you delight yourself in the Lord, wisdom abounds, and the man (or woman) who fears the Lord obtains great blessing and wealth. Why is this so important for us to see? Because we *all* have a mindset about money (wealth)—how to make money, how money works, the relationship we have with money and wealth, and what we have heard all of our lives growing up about money. It shapes our relationship with money.

Over 75% of the small business owners and entrepreneurs I have coached throughout my career come to me with a definite **lack mindset** about money, and don't realize it. They definitely don't realize that they are hindering their own business and financial growth. This includes people who have money and those who don't. Even some pastors I coach—who preach regularly on giving and abundance—have a deep-rooted seed that somehow, for some reason, **great blessing and wealth are not for them**. They believe God is no respecter of persons, but for one reason or another, they feel it's not meant for *them*.

Where does this *'lack mindset'* come from?

It is a deep-rooted belief that was heard, seen, or told by family, friends, the enemy, or your own inner critic. It is a seed planted that sounds like this:

- "Don't you wish we were born into a wealthy family?"
- "You'll have to work for every penny you ever make."
- "You'll never get ahead."
- "Being rich is for other people, not me."
- "You'll never be smart enough to be rich–you don't have enough education."

- "You wouldn't know what to do with money if you had it."
- "Wealth and riches are for other people, not me."
- "We're blessed—but having money or talking about making money isn't humble."
- "God doesn't like that, so I shouldn't talk about having money."
- "If I get money or do something great, I won't take any credit for it because that's pride."
- "We'll always be blessed just enough to make it and that's okay– I don't deserve more than that."

It's okay to make money, have money, and build a wildly successful business, ministry, church, and organization. Just remember who taught you, opened doors for you, and surrounded you with favor. "And you shall remember the Lord your God, for *it is* He who gives you power **to get wealth**, that He may **establish His covenant** which He swore to your fathers, as *it is* this day.

She is filled with blessings and wealth, not only because she is gifted, but because she is grounded.

Her business flourishes not only because of strategy, but because of stance—a **stance** rooted in integrity, honor, generosity, and righteousness.

Integrity is the invisible currency of the Kingdom. It is what clients remember, partners respect, and Heaven rewards.

The Psalmist reveals the secret: **Blessing and wealth fill the house of the wise BECAUSE her integrity endures.**

Others, but most of all heaven sees her faithfulness in the little things.

They witness her truthfulness, her fairness, her refusal to cut corners or compromise.

Her yes means yes—her no means no.

Her business dealings are pure and right.

She honors the Word above the world.

She puts Scripture before sales.

She chooses character over shortcuts.

She understands that **integrity is a seed—and God always multiplies it.**

She is not only a businesswoman—she is a minister of reconciliation in the marketplace.

She carries in her the gospel as she works; therefore her ethics, her attitude, her conversations, and her compassion guide her business dealings. She is a Proverbs 31 Woman. She is a seller of purple like Lydia, clothed in the precious blood of Jesus.

She is generous—quick to give, quick to help the poor, quick to minister to the broken.

She is diligent, not distracted—devoted, not divided.

She chases hard after God; because of that she never has to chase success—**it chases her.**

Wealth takes up residence in her home.

Blessing is her fountain—she overflows with wisdom.

An entrepreneurial woman of faith doesn't succeed by manipulation, striving, or networking alone—**but because of her virtue, vigor, and vision.**

"Wealth follows wisdom, and wisdom produces integrity. When you follow hard after God, blessings and wealth will find your address."

— Dr. Margo Bush

Faith Action

Do a personal integrity check in your business:

- Review your contracts, communication, service, billing, and follow-through.
- Identify **one place** where you can raise the standard of excellence and integrity.
- Ask the Lord to make you trustworthy in the eyes of Heaven and in the eyes of people.

Reflection Questions

1. In what areas of my business can I increase virtue, vigor, and vision?
2. What does "integrity that endures" look like in my daily work?
3. Do people see honesty and integrity through the way I conduct my life and business?

Prayer Prompt

"Heavenly Father, help me to walk in integrity in every area of my life and business. Let my actions reflect Your character. Fill my home and my work with blessings, wealth, purpose, and favor. Create in me a clean heart, O Lord, and make me a vessel of reconciliation and grace

in the marketplace. May my actions be filled with integrity, and my life bring honor to Your name.

In Jesus' name, Amen."

Scripture References

"[1] Shout in celebration of praise to the Lord! Everyone who loves the Lord and delights in him will cherish his words and be blessed beyond expectation. [2] Their descendants will be prosperous and influential. Every generation of the righteous will experience his favor. [3] Great blessing and wealth fills the house of the wise, for their integrity endures forever."

—Psalm 112:1–3 (TPT)

"He that walketh uprightly walketh surely."

—Proverbs 10:9 (KJV)

"Honor the Lord…so shall thy barns be filled with plenty."

—Proverbs 3:9–10 (KJV)

She Means Business Declaration

- I declare that I walk every day in integrity and because of that blessing and wealth fill my house.

- I seek the Lord's wisdom in every business decision.

- Favor surrounds me, generosity flows through me and because I work diligently, my house is filled with great blessings and wealth.

About the Author

Dr. Margo Bush

Founder of Legacy Christian University | Business & Church Growth Strategist

Dr. Margo Bush is a dynamic voice for Christian women in business, inspiring a global movement of faith-driven entrepreneurs to build thriving, profitable, and Kingdom-impacting organizations. A successful entrepreneur, speaker, educator, growth coach, and Senior Business Analyst, Dr. Margo brings decades of experience empowering business leaders, ministry teams, and entrepreneurs to grow with excellence, integrity, and purpose.

She holds a Doctorate of Theology and Ministry, an Associate of Arts in Music and Theater, and is a certified Senior Business Analyst through Global Resources, North America's largest small business consulting firm.

Dr. Margo is the author of *Dream Big, Live Big! The Basics of Growing a Thriving Small Business* and *The Shift Administration Resource Manual*—a strategic guide for church leadership and organizational growth. Her passion for leadership development and business innovation has led her to coach entrepreneurs across diverse industries, consult executive pastors and their teams, and share stages with top leaders around the world.

As host of *The Dr. Margo Show*—a podcast that connects authors, innovators, and influencers to new audiences—she continues to expand

her reach, helping others embrace bold vision and unstoppable faith in business and ministry.

After the sudden loss of her husband, Dr. Margo transformed their small printing and publishing company into a thriving organization to serve authors, speakers, and visionaries. Her story of resilience, reinvention, and business success fuels her mission to equip others with the education, mindset, and tools needed to learn how to earn more, create financial security, and grow organizations with a mission.

As the founder of **Legacy Christian University, Don't Do Business Alone Coaching Firm, Don't Do Church Alone, and Bush Publishing & Associates**, she mentors leaders to scale with strategy, strengthen brand identity, and build organizations with a purpose for Kingdom Impact..

Rooted in Oklahoma, Dr. Margo blends faith, business acumen, and a contagious passion to raise up a generation of successful leaders, Kingdom-minded entrepreneurs, and women who lead with vision and build with purpose. She is the proud mother of two sons and "Gigi" to five beautiful grandchildren. When she's not coaching or speaking, you'll find her playing piano, singing Opera, or watching the dolphins early in the morning in the bay.

Available
Books and Curriculum
by Margo Bush

She Means Business: Faith & Prosperity for Women in Business

Dream Big, Live Big!

Dream Big, Live Big Companion Study Guide

LCU Executive Business Certificate Program

LCU School of Entrepreneurship

LCU School of Biblical Studies & Ministry

LCU Church Growth Certificate Program

Visit BushPublishing.com to order books and materials by Margo Bush

LCU Certificate & Degree Programs visit LegacyChristianIniversity.com

Find all products and courses by Dr. Margo Bush at MargoBush.com

Visit LegacyChristianUniversity.com for more information about Dr. Margo Bush, Founder & President

"What the world calls business, God calls ministry. You carry His assignment into your industry and His influence into the marketplace."

—Dr. Margo Bush

Recommended Reading

BOOKS

The E-Myth Revisited: *Why Most Small Businesses Don't Work and What to Do About It—A Guide to Starting a Business in a Productive and Successful Way*—by Michael Gerber

Guerilla Marketing—by Jay Conrad Levinson

Chasing the Lion, In a Pit On a Snowy Day, The Circle Maker, and ***The Circle Maker-Devotional***—by Mark Batterson

She Means Business, and ***Dream Big Live Big***—by Margo Bush

How to Influence People—by John Maxwell

How to Win Friends and Influence People, and ***How to Stop Worrying and Start Living***—by Dale Carnegie

The Art of the Deal—by Donald Trump

The Ten-Day MBA: *A Step-by-Step Guide to Mastering the Skills Taught In America's Top Business Schools*—by Steven A. Silbiger

Winning at the Sport of Business: *If I Can Do It, You Can Do It*—by Mark Cuban

The Power of One More: *The Ultimate Guide to Happiness and Success*—by Ed Mylett

The Wisdom of Walt: *Leadership Lessons from the Happiest Place on Earth*—by Jeffrey A. Barnes

Traction: *Get a Grip on Your Business*—by Gino Wickman

Churchill: *Walking with Destiny*—by Andrew Roberts

Build a Business You Love: *Mastering the Five Stages of Business*—by Dave Ramsey

The Zappos Experience: *5 Principles to Inspire, Engage, and Wow*—by Joseph Michelli

And David Perceived He Was King: *Identity—The Key to Your Destiny*—by Dale L. Mast

Ultra Marathon Man: *Confession of an All-Night Runner*—by Dean Karnazes

For Such a Time as This: *My Faith Journey Through the White House and Beyond*—by Kayleigh McEnany

Never Split the Difference: *Negotiating as if Your Life Depended on It*—by Chris Voss

See You at the Top—by Zig Ziglar

The Warren Buffet Way—by Robert Hagstrom

The Secret Life of Words: *English Words and Their Origins*—by Anne Curzan

The Road Back to You: *An Enneagram Journey to Self-Discovery*—by Ian Morgan Cron and Suzanne Stabile

Think and Grow Rich—by Napoleon Hill

Goals: *How to Get Everything You Want Faster Than You Ever Thought Possible*—by Brian Tracy

The Seven Habits of Highly Effective People: *Powerful Lessons in Personal Change*—by Stephen R. Covey

Recommended Reading

Magazines

Success Magazine—visit www.success.com to subscribe.

Entrepreneur Magazine—visit www.entrepreneur.com to subscribe.

LEGACY CHRISTIAN UNIVERSITY
Accredited and Online

LCU Degrees and Certificate Programs

TRAINING STUDENTS IN HIGHER EDUCATION

School of Entrepreneurship, B.A.
Biblical Studies & Ministry, B.A.
Proforming Arts, A.A.
Music & Theater, A.A.
AI Technology, A.A.
Audio Engineering,
Certificate and more...

Consider Helping a Student
Become a 818 Legacy Sponsor Today!
Scan the QR code to donate

JOIN US 2026 SCHOOL YEAR

Apply at
LegacyChristianUniversity.com

bush PUBLISHING & associates
BushPublishing.com

BECOME A PUBLISHED AUTHOR AND EXPERIENCE BUSH PUBLISHING UNIQUE DIFFERENCE WE PARTNER WITH OUR AUTHORS TO GET THEM NOTICED

WE WANT TO WORK WITH YOU

BushPublishing.com
Call us: 405-492-2805

www.ingramcontent.com/pod-product-compliance
Lightning Source LLC
Chambersburg PA
CBHW070055080526
44586CB00013B/1061